Gottheil

MOHAMMED

Mohammed

BY R. F. DIBBLE

THE VIKING PRESS
NEW YORK · : · MCMXXVI

PRINTED IN U. S. A.

CONTENTS

MOHAMMED

". . . it may perhaps be expected that I should balance his faults and virtues, that I should decide whether the title of enthusiast or impostor more properly belongs to that extraordinary man. Had I been intimately conversant with the son of Abdallah, the task would still be difficult, and the success uncertain: at the distance of twelve centuries, I darkly contemplate his shade through a cloud of religious incense; and, could I truly delineate the portrait of an hour, the fleeting resemblance would not equally apply to the solitary of Mount Hira, to the preacher of Mecca, and to the conqueror of Arabia."

—GIBBON

I

ARABIA: FELIX, PETRÆA ET DESERTA

I

MIDWAY between Asia and Africa lies the giant peninsula of Arabia—the vast, immutable, resplendently mysterious country that bridges the Orient and the Occident. Shaped somewhat like a triangle and somewhat like an oblong, she appears to the vulgar eye more like a boot with its toe lopped off. Three bodies of water—the Red Sea, the Arabian Sea, and the Persian Gulf—roll their guardian waves against her rocky, mountainous coasts, while her northern domain is staunchly defended by the impassable Syrian Desert.

Perhaps no other country, not even Switzerland, has been so well protected by nature against the assaults—military, economic or religious—of the outside world. Before the seventh century, the fury of the Roman legions and the enthusiasm of martial Christians had been expended in prodigious but wholly futile efforts to subjugate her: the one because its soldiers died of heat and thirst in her almost uninhabitable interior, and the other because its votaries too often restricted their religious zeal to a general consumption of alcohol and to an individual union with more than one wife or concubine. But in any case, inasmuch as the Arabs were fierce and warlike by nature, and were acquainted with such refinements of wine and concupiscence as even the most aspiring Christians had not achieved, the attacks of Pagan Rome and Christian Palestine would probably have come to naught. Even to this day, indeed, Arabia has been left almost entirely alone by the outside world. Timeless, changeless and unromantic save to the capricious imagination of poets and travelers, her interminable, ocean-like billows of arid sand have saved her from all conquests. As she was in the dim and remote beginnings of history, so she largely remains; and the modern wanderer who penetrates her obscure interior cannot be certain whether he will be greeted with affluent hospitality or a frowning hostility that may prove inimical to life itself.

A land of contrasts! Three-fourths surrounded by water, her extensive interior is a scorched and stony desert; her verdant southern coasts are soon lost in a lifeless and almost level plateau; her abundantly fertile province of Yemen, known to romance as Araby the Blest, fades northward into the ominous wastes of Nejd, or Arabia Deserta, and northwestward into the precipitous wilds of Hejaz, or Arabia Petræa. Short rivers hurl their jagged torrents down her sloping sides, while prolific oases, always placid and unruffled, dot her deserts. The fragrant breezes that come from the Indian Ocean are quickly assimilated into the stagnant, oppressive atmosphere of her centre; her palmy springs may teem with sweet and pure waters, or with saline, sulphurous scum. The broiling rays of the midday sun give way nightly to bitter and frosty dews; her long-slumbering sands are at times whirled violently aloft by sharp, sudden, blinding storms that often overwhelm caravans and tents, to subside as suddenly, leaving her surface forever different—and yet forever the same. A land untouched by time, where time's oppression is yet most powerfully felt; a land that never alters, though perpetually subject to alteration; a land where the new is eternally old, and the old is eternally new.

Nor does the paradox confine itself to her terrain; her inhabitants and their social institutions, particularly during the seventh century, exhibited corresponding discrepancies. Although all Arabs were ruled by nearly identical codes of honor, morals and manners, spoke a generic tongue, and were passionately patriotic, they were yet divided into tribes that bowed before countless fetishes, conversed in individual dialects, and were ever ready to fight to the death for the supremacy of their particular clan. At times of national danger, it is true, they fervently abandoned all local prejudices in a tumultuous display of chauvinism; but such contingencies were rare and, since the vague, immemorial inception of her history, Arabian tribes, on the slightest pretext or on no pretext at all, had frequently plunged with limitless enthusiasm into the gratifying job of slitting fraternal throats. All these various tribes, moreover, were grouped into two fairly distinct divisions: the city-dwellers and the Bedouins.

From her earliest days, Arabia had depended on caravan trade for her subsistence. In the times of Abraham, Moses and Solomon, her traders had carried the fragrant spices and other products of Palestine and Arabia—cassia, cinnamon, frankincense, myrrh, gums, leather and coffee—into Egypt; and, conversely, the "Kings of Arabia" had also freighted into Judea and their own beloved land the priceless rarities of the Orient: ivory, ebony and precious gems. For the dangers of ocean commerce made a land route absolutely essential for the exchange of merchandise between the East and the West, and Arabia alone supplied the necessary bridge for this extensive barter. Caravans from every nation, therefore, had for centuries passed each other on her sere surface; her oases had thus become cynosures where rest and refreshment could be had; and so by degrees these centres of repose became the sites where marts, temples and sanctuaries sprang indiscriminately up. These nuclei of elementary civilizations led, little by little, to the development of an urban population where those Arabs who chanced to be disposed toward peace and business could lead a moderately serene life. But the instinct of nomadism was incalculably strong in most of Arabia's sons, and myriads of men, yielding to the powerful atavistic impulse, gladly relinquished the relatively soft environment of urbanism in order to undergo, with fatalistic indifference, the hazards of a roaming, marauding, desert life.

These Bedouins, "dwellers in the open land" or "people of the tent," were at once independent and servile, patriotic and anarchistic, friendly and hostile, thievish and chivalric. A contemptuous impatience of restraints and bonds of any kind made each one of them look upon himself as a king; at the same time each one willingly bowed the knee to the precepts of the most powerful ruler, or sheik, who, through the prestige of inherent or acquired power, automatically guided the shifting destinies of each clan. Their strongest institution was the blood-feud—quickly abandoned, to be sure, when a common enemy appeared on the horizon—and tribal warfare or personal strife was an every-day affair; nevertheless, the centralizing power arising from perpetual traditions of a mutual fraternalism of interests held these roving hordes in an elastic coalescence.

The stranger who sought the hospitality of their tents might be greeted by a flashing scimitar or a handclasp and a hearty dinner—he could never tell which fate would be his, except by experiment. If he were successful, he was naturally pleased; whereas, if he failed, his opinion and his life were soon of no moment to anyone save the Bedouins who took his booty. Equally sensitive to insults or compliments, they guarded above all else the honor of their beards and their women: to shake the one was to invite immediate death, and to cast the smallest aspersion on the other was to embrace a corresponding doom. And still, despite the obeisance paid to women, the birth of a daughter was looked upon as a horrible misfortune. The burial alive of female infants was a common custom, and the natural death of one brought hearty congratulations to the fortunate parents; while such girls as managed to remain alive until their seventh or eighth year were summarily disposed of at that tender age to the first suitor who appeared. Women, in brief, were mere chattel: the eldest son commonly inherited his father's wives as a logical and desirable portion of the parental estate.

Their livelihood was won principally by the robbing of caravans. The plundering of them, in fact, was justly held by the Bedouins to be merely a righteous method of exacting the customs that were levied everywhere; for the land, they maintained, was exclusively theirs by right of domain, and trespassers thereon must pay an appropriate penalty. Mounted upon their swift and spirited horses, sprung from the purest pedigree through many generations of careful selection and trained to respond instantly to the slightest touch of the rein, the Bedouins rarely failed to overtake their fleeing prey. Since the loot of caravans supplied them with all the necessities of life, they naturally worshiped their horses and camels—in particular the ones they had stolen—with a superstitious reverence. Their dromedaries, indeed, offered an escape from every contingency: they furnished transportation, food (both tender flesh and milk), long hair for tent-building, and, in case of a pinch, the water in their capacious reservoirs could be used for drink and their dung for fuel. The supreme height of generosity for a Bedouin was attained on those very rare occasions when he slaughtered his own cherished camel to feed and warm the stranger of a night.

In some respects the most striking and potent social institution among the Arabs, urbanites and nomads alike, was the annual fair. Every year, during certain months that were supposed to be inviolably sacred—so sacred, in fact, that even personal and tribal broils were taboo—a series of pageants was held throughout the whole country; but the most populous and successful of them all was celebrated at Ukaz, near Mecca. To that place came Arabia's best and fairest: opulent merchants, actors garbed in masks or veils, poets of the desert, sheiks notorious for their proficiency in war and love, dancing girls, and maidens whose alluring sensuousness was subtly dissembled in languorous modesty, met on a common footing. Specimens of trade and primitive art abounded in many booths; the violent contortions of the corybantes, as they whirled dizzily from tent to tent, excited the reckless Bedouins to such a pitch that drunken orgies occasionally followed, during which the sacred season was momentarily forgotten and resolutions of peace and chastity conveniently overlooked. The pious devotions of pilgrims, the piteous moans of beggars for alms, and the quiet exchange of talk between traders, sightseers and friends, was often disturbed by hilarious shrieks of applause for the bacchantes, by the clang of the cymbal, and the clash of the scimitar. If shrines for prayer were open all day, gambling houses did a flourishing business at night; and if poetic and histrionic contests delighted the onlookers, unfortunate results frequently followed. For the poets, chanting a rudely rhythmical verse, incontinently boasted their individual excellence in the manufacture of stanzas; and not seldom did they caustically satirize the members of some other clan, meanwhile boundlessly extolling the bravery of their own warriors and the surpassing beauty and chastity of their women. All this bloated braggadocio paved the way to feuds between different tribes, and thus the fairs, which were supposed to allay hatreds and inculcate friendships, often led to results that were precisely opposite. Thus, for weeks and even months, the glittering, gorgeously colored spectacle went on—a dazzling drama that, in its violent contrasts of mystical adoration and wanton lechery, of humility and gross egotism, of entrancing beauty and fetid squalor, furnishes perhaps the best clue to the complex and divergent character of Arabia's children.

Her religion was an all-pervading form of indigenous and manifold idolatry, tinctured with faint traces of Judaism and Christianity. The worship of the stars, that furnished a nightly quota of detached beauty and —what was more important—utility as a never-failing compass, is easily understandable; but just why she should have reverenced the blazing tropical sun and the tons upon tons of stones that were sprinkled over her parched surface, tempts to a metaphysical speculation which—as certain learned dissertations prove—is more fascinating than illuminating. Perhaps the most original and poetic element in this idol-worship was a vague belief in the Jinn: those vast, inchoate, awe-inspiring creatures, now friendly and now inimical, that—so every devout Arab believed—brooded like gigantic birds in the illimitable heavens that canopied Arabia. Judaism had made some effort to proselytize the Arabs, but had wisely given up the attempt after it realized what fascinating opportunities existed for the profits of trade. Christian Abyssinia, too, had manifested a laudable desire to turn her Pagan neighbor to the right way; but proud and impetuous Arabs were not particularly susceptible to the pleas of negroes, even though they chanced to be Christian negroes; and besides, the dialectical hair-splittings which so enthralled the followers of Arius and Athanasius could hardly be expected to offer much interest to minds that unfortunately had never been given an opportunity to become enraptured by the intricate charms of theology. But, in common with the devotees of Moses and Christ, the Arabs exalted ancestor-worship, and they even claimed, with a faith as touching as it was irrelevant, that Abraham himself was one of their most distinguished forefathers.

Here, then, was a land of marvelous opportunity for the right man. Ruled by rigid taboos and certain patriarchs of exceptional prowess, yet actually without a ruler; devoutly religious as religion goes, yet without a unifying religion; containing an enormous amount of military valor, yet wasting her strength in inter-tribal battles—Arabia, in the seventh century, stood in dire dearth of some commanding personality. The consecutive dominions of Egypt, Assyria, Persia and Greece—nations that had once been supreme in regal splendor—had disintegrated in rapid succession; and Rome, the mightiest of them all, was now nearing her eclipse. Neither Syria nor Persia was of much account any longer, Africa was weak, the Christians had forgotten Christ in their absorption in the more thrilling pursuit of schismatic squabbling, and the Jews too often bartered their sacred phylacteries for the products of Pagan ingenuity. Meanwhile, during the kaleidoscopic evolution and disruption of world-conquering empires, Arabia had dragged out only a ghostly existence; she was a nation that had either been carelessly forgotten or contemptuously disregarded; she had won no place in the sun. The general decadence of nations and faiths at this time offered an unparalleled chance to the mythical Arab who, by evolving a religious and political system based upon the common elements that formed the solid foundation of every Arabian tribe, should fuse the emotional and economic strength of the land into an indivisible unity, and—who knew?—perhaps carry on the torch recently dropped by the expiring Roman Empire. Now, as careful students of history are well aware, great men, whether warriors, statesmen or prophets, have a way of bobbing up at the precise moment when they are most needed. So it happened that, in the city of Mecca, probably in August in the year 570, Mohammed, the Prophet of Allah, was born.

II

For centuries before the birth of the Prophet, Mecca had been the most populous and influential city in Arabia. She owed this eminence to two very different things: to her geographical situation, and to some pretty legends that sought to explain her divine origin.

In the first place, she occupied a convenient and highly strategic position on a great caravan route. She reposed in a natural amphitheatre, partially encompassed by precipitous hills of quartz and granite; touching her southern border lay the pleasant plains of Yemen, while her northern edge was overhung by the lowering rocks of Hejaz. The never-failing well, Zemzem, that gushed from her centre furnished an apparently inexhaustible supply of water for the passing trains of merchandise; it became a refreshing stopping place, and thus by degrees grew to be a focus for commerce. Crowds of traders, coming principally from Yemen, eventually located there and established the beginnings of a mercantile business: they collected the frontier customs, the hire for hauling produce, the dues arising from protection, and, in addition, they started various types of traffic among themselves.

Orthodox Arabs, however, prefer to explain her superiority by giving more credit to her miraculous inception than to dry economic matters. According to them, when Hagar was expelled into the wilderness she chanced in her wanderings to come into the vale of Mecca. Both she and little Ishmael were almost overcome with thirst, when the child accidentally kicked the ground in a paroxysm of passion, and lo! a stream of pure water bubbled forth from the spot struck by his dainty toes. When Abraham heard of this miracle he visited the place, and, aided by his dutiful son Ishmael, now grown to manhood, built a sacred temple and instituted definite rites of pilgrimage. Inasmuch as the Arabs had mingled with the Hebrew race for many generations on matters of business, it was perhaps natural enough that they should have relied on the Jews for a superior facility in poetical imagination as well as a superior business credit.

Whichever explanation is more plausible, there is no doubt that, even before the beginning of the Christian era, Mecca was a well-established mercantile city that included a sacred temple, the Kaba, which was already a national centre of adoration. At some early date there was instituted a carefully systematized, two-fold form of worship based upon well-tried Hebrew models: the Lesser and Greater Pilgrimages. Devotees who were able to satisfy their consciences by performing the ritual of the Lesser Pilgrimage only, went about it thus: they came to Mecca, generally during the sacred month of Rejeb, feverishly kissed the blessed Black Stone—the most divinely hallowed rock in a country that reverenced every one of her millions of stones—imbedded in the eastern corner of the Kaba, sedately walked seven times around the saintly edifice, and then marched in a more hasty manner seven times to and fro between two spots near by, over a route which Hagar was supposed to have trod. But the Greater Pilgrimage demanded a more strenuous faith. Those who elected to perform its stricter stipulations could do so only during the month of Dhul-Hijja, which was even more holy than Rejeb; and, besides accomplishing the requirements already specified, they were obliged to travel on foot to Arafat, a small hill some twelve miles east of Mecca, and to struggle manfully up its steep sides. Before entering the hallowed territory of Mecca, the votaries of both pilgrimages donned a special raiment, and, when all the religious activities were completed, they shaved their heads and pared their nails.

Favored thus by nature and superstition, Mecca had grown apace. For centuries different clans vied with each other in an effort to gain control of her destiny—a control that was eminently desirable, for by the fifth century Mecca was *Mecca,* in the most modern sense of the word. The dialect spoken by her citizens had come to be regarded as the standard of purity by which all other tribes were judged; and pilgrims from every extraneous Arabian clan, except the untamable Bedouins, came yearly to pay their vows and drink from the sacred fount of Zemzem—whose waters were a bit brackish, to be sure, but still satisfactorily sacred. During that century a sect called the Koreish finally won a foothold that gave every evidence of being permanent. Despite occasional bickerings among themselves as to matters of patronage and patriarchal succession, they always agreed when an outside enemy appeared; and successive victories over those who vainly sought to supplant them led to their exaltation throughout all Arabia.

Elated with the pride of successful conquest, the Koreish were not slow to reap the fruits of power. Although the sanctity of the holy city induced a general atmosphere of peace, forays and brawls occasionally took place, and the Koreish merchants therefore conceived the scheme of wearing badges that kept them moderately safe from assault. But measures of defence soon gave way to offence: "Let us release ourselves from some of the observances imposed upon the multitude," they said. So they solaced themselves by undergoing the rites of the Lesser Pilgrimage only; they refused to be restricted to the use of the plain butter and cheese that formed the staple pilgrim diet; they adopted the luxury of leathern tents instead of those made from camel-hair. Finally, they formulated stringent rules to be observed by all pilgrims except themselves—rules that smack more of economic pressure than unalloyed faith. All outsiders were forbidden to bring food within the walls of Mecca, and were forced to circumnavigate the Kaba entirely naked or dressed in clothes that could be obtained only from the Meccan merchants. In view of these facts, there can be but little doubt that a prophet who would invent and promulgate a more pure and magnanimous faith was very desirable.

II

EARLY YEARS

I

AMONG the numberless misty matters that befog the career of Mohammed is the moot question of his parentage. The voice of Allah, speaking through the lips of his Prophet in the Koran, proclaims that his best beloved son was an orphan, poor and astray; but, while a proper modesty may well make one hesitate to question the smallest decree of such a transcendent authority, one can still scarcely refrain from noting that most boys who attain a position of unrivaled eminence in later life are prone to give a suspicious amount of emphasis to the hardships of their youth. Practically everything that concerns the life of the Prophet is flecked with more or less obscurity—an obscurity that has been intensified by both his friends and his foes. Almost all the Christian commentators have dwelt lovingly upon the worst elements in the life and teachings of Mohammed, and the numerous cliques of Arabs who whined or rebelled against his imperial sway swelled the chorus of malignant defamation; his followers, on the contrary, have been guilty of the most fanatical panegyrics. Buffeted and disfigured between these two intensely antagonistic forces of opinion, the massive figure of Mohammed must forever remain largely ambiguous and enigmatical. His Boswells were too Boswellian, and his Froudes were too Froudish. And yet, by steering a zigzag course between the Scylla of rhapsodical praise and the Charybdis of envious detraction, it may be possible to arrive at a relatively detached and peaceful haven where the immeasurable Arab looms a little less vaguely through the remoteness of thirteen centuries.

There seems to be little doubt that he was descended from those lofty Koreish whose opposition, which at first nearly succeeded in holding his name in perpetual oblivion, eventually caused him to emerge into the light of deathless fame. For a century and a half, his forefathers had been rulers among the Koreish. In the middle of the fifth century, Kosai, his ancestor at the fifth remove, had won the distinction of being the first man to advance the Koreish to a position of supremacy over Mecca. At his death his three sons fought for the honor of succeeding him; but Abd Menaf won out, and was followed in turn by Hashim—rich, amorous, charitable, glorious Hashim!—and his son Abd Al-Muttalib, the estimable grandfather of the Prophet.

When Abd Al-Muttalib came into power early in

the sixth century, he fell at first upon evil days. Certain of the Koreish were unfriendly, the caravan business had been in a bad way for some time, and the holy water of Zemzem, no longer used as of yore, had choked up and was almost forgotten. Abd Al-Muttalib, who well knew the traditions of its ancient glory, and who found it difficult to get enough water from lesser Meccan wells for visiting pilgrims, instituted a laborious search for the venerable stonework which was known to have surrounded it. Finally his virtuous efforts were rewarded, and, aided by his son Al-Harith, he began to scoop out the debris with which it was clogged. As he neared the bottom, he came upon the two golden gazelles, and the swords and suits of armor, that had been buried there by a Jurhumite king three centuries before as a suitable hiding place against the despoliations of his enemies. The Koreish, hearing of Abd Al-Muttalib's lucky find, immediately demanded a share of the booty. It was finally agreed that the dispute should be settled by the casting of lots: one for Abd Al-Muttalib, one for the Koreish, and—inasmuch as all parties concerned in the row were religiously minded—one for the Kaba. Abd Al-Muttalib got the swords and armor, the Kaba got the gazelles, and the Koreish got nothing. That very day, indeed, dated their gradual defection from the faith of their fathers; but Abd Al-Muttalib, in an excess of grateful devotion, beat the gazelles into plates of gold with which he decorated the interior door of the Kaba, and, in a similar excess of caution, added a golden lock and key to the door. His faith was properly rewarded, for from that day the waters of Zemzem again flowed without interruption; and so Abd Al-Muttalib grew in social, financial and religious strength, and became the father of many pious and powerful sons. And yet—such a wayward and capricious dame is Clio!—there are those who aver that Mohammed's grandfather was not the leading Meccan of his time, and that most of the stories connected with his name are fabulous inventions of the Prophet's hero-worshiping satellites.

Fortunately, all parties seem agreed that Abdallah, the youngest and most favored son of Abd Al-Muttalib, was the unambiguous sire of Mohammed. The ways of Allah are not less perplexing than the ways of God, and it appears probable that, had it not been for the direct intervention of the whimsical Arabian Deity, Abdallah would have perished before he had begotten his extraordinary son. During the early years of Abd Al-Muttalib, when he had but one son to aid him in his struggles against his political opponents, he had vowed that, should he ever be favored with ten sons, he would sacrifice one of them to the Deity. This vow—rash enough for any young man, and rashest of all, perhaps, for an Arab—was in the course of time providentially fulfilled; and when lots were cast by the obedient Abd Al-Muttalib, the fatal die fell upon Abdallah, his pet boy. The hitherto invincible faith of Abd Al-Muttalib was tremendously shaken; his weeping daughters—for Allah had been more than generous—also besought him to cast lots between Abdallah and ten camels: the conventional substitute for human bloodshed. For nine successive times the arrow pointed toward Abdallah—could it be that Allah was inexorable? At each throw ten additional camels had been added to the previous number until, on the tenth throw, they amounted to an even hundred. Then at last Allah, who was presumably far more interested in the birth of Mohammed than in a wilderness of camels, relented and released his faithful servant from his oath. Thus a hundred camels perished beneath the sacrificial knife, Abd Al-Muttalib's piety was recompensed, Abdallah was saved, and the miraculous birth of the Prophet was assured.

It came about thus. Toward the end of 569, Abd Al-Muttalib had betrothed Abdallah to a Meccan maiden named Amina; and at the same time, even though he was over seventy and Allah had abundantly granted his youthful plea for potency, he himself had married a radiantly youthful cousin of Amina's. Some months later Mecca was invaded by an army under Abraha, a Christian warrior from Abyssinia, who brought an elephant in his train—a prodigy that so astounded the simple Arabs that the year of the invasion was ever after called "the Elephant." He had come, he said, merely to destroy the impious Kaba, and he had no desire to shed any man's blood; but inasmuch as the Meccans knew that Christian Abraha's fervor had already manifested itself in the plunder of hundreds of camels, they were rightly sceptical of any promise whatever on his part. Overtures of peace were unsuccessful, for on no account would the wealthy Koreish agree to permit the demolition of their most remunerative mercantile house, and preparations were accordingly made to offer some feeble resistance to the invader. Then Abd Al-Muttalib bethought himself of a possible means to thwart the impending peril. Leaning on the door of the Kaba, he prayed aloud thus: "Defend, O Lord, thine own house, and suffer not the Cross to triumph over the Kaba!" He then made haste to join the other refugees, who had betaken themselves to the neighboring crags to watch whatever might betide. Sharp-eared Allah, aloof in his own particular Heaven, heard the prayer and promptly answered it by inflicting a pestilential disease upon the raiding Christian hosts. Overwhelmed by the disaster, they began a confused retreat: hundreds of them died by the wayside, and Abraha himself, covered with a mass of poisonous and putrid ulcers, soon expired in terrible agony. Thus was the Kaba gloriously saved and the Cross ignominiously overthrown—an event so prophetical of coming centuries that its portentous symbolism demanded an incarnate manifestation. The routed Christian warriors had barely left the shores of Arabia when Amina gave birth to a son.

II

His advent, we are told, was decorously surrounded by all manner of signs and omens. The travail of Amina was entirely painless; earthquakes loosed the bowels of mountains and caused great bodies of water, whose names were unfortunately not specified, to wither away or overflow; the sacred fire of Zoroaster which, under the jealous care of the Magi, had spouted ceaseless flames for nearly a thousand years, was summarily extinguished; indeed, all the idols in the world —except, presumably, the Kaba—unceremoniously tumbled from their exalted places. Immediately after the babe was born an ethereal light dazzled the surrounding territory, and, on the very moment when his eyes were first opened, he lifted them to Heaven and exclaimed: "God is great! There is no God but Allah and I am His Prophet!" All these poetic fancies have been appropriately denounced by Christian scribes, who have claimed that nature would never have dignified the birth of a Pagan like Mohammed with such marvelous prodigies as indubitably attended the advent and crucifixion of Christ.

In the meantime a tragedy of much moment had occurred. High-spirited Abdallah—the lovely youth whose charms were so compelling that two hundred languishing virgins are said to have perished from jealous disappointment on his wedding night—was already no more. After remaining with his bride for the customary period of three days, he had departed on a business engagement to Gaza; but, on the return trip, he had sickened and died at Medina. The period of mourning for him was barely over when his posthumous son was born. Grief-stricken Abd Al-Muttalib, who was still bewailing his dead son in the repose of the Kaba, was so comforted when Amina's messenger brought him the glad tidings that he at once headed a procession of relatives to visit his latest grandchild. With the tender babe in his arms, he immediately returned to the Kaba, and, standing beside its holy altar, he gave thanks to Allah for his mercies and benefits. One week later Abd Al-Muttalib gave a feast in honor of the child; and during the course of the festivities the aged ruler presaged an unspeakably glorious destiny for his grandson as the dawning leader of his race, and concluded his remarks by christening him Mohammed, "the Praised."

Since the suckling of their own children was not considered to be a proper vocation for high-born Arab women, Amina, as a descendant of the lordly Koreish, rightly refused to nurse her child. For the first few days of his precarious existence he was nourished by Thuweiba, a slave of his own uncle, Abu Lahab; yet, in spite of the brevity of this experience, it is confidently claimed that Mohammed never forgot it, and that so long as he lived he regularly sent her clothes and other gifts. A new nurse then had to be found. According to some fairly authentic traditions, he spent his first five years among the Bedouins under the care of a foster-mother named Halima. At the age of two he was weaned and taken back to his mother; but she was so pleased with her lusty-looking baby that she said: "Take him with thee back again to the desert; for I fear the unhealthy air of Mecca." After two more years the robust but high-strung boy, who, like most embryo prophets, had an acutely sensitive nervous system, showed signs of what was probably an epileptic attack. His foster-parents were so disturbed that they at once took him home; and only by the greatest efforts was Amina able to assuage their fears—were not most children normally subject to worms or the croup?—and persuade them to take him back to the desert. So great was their love for the youngster that they did so; but a year later they were again frightened by recurrent symptoms, and the five-year-old boy was then definitely restored to his mother, with whom he remained for nearly another year. Amina then took him to Medina, where his father's maternal relatives dwelt; for she felt all a mother's delight in showing off the pretty and playful tricks of her little son. But another momentous tragedy now impended. About a month later she died; and thus Mohammed, at the age of six, was left an orphan.

Had the lad's parents, or even one of them, lived until his maturity! In either case, incalculable results might have followed: there might have been no Prophet, no Koran, no Islam—one is tempted to say that there might have been no Allah. But they died; and for the next two years the bereaved boy was cared for by Abd Al-Muttalib, who loved him with all the partiality of age. Sometimes, as the old patriarch sat at ease on a rug shaded from the sun, Mohammed would peremptorily usurp his seat. Then the old man's sons would try to push the little rascal off, but Abd Al-Muttalib would say, "Let my little son alone!" and, baked by the burning sun, would pet Mohammed and feast his ears on the childish shouts and gurgles of the victor.

Two years later Abd Al-Muttalib went to join Abdallah and Amina, and Mohammed, weeping bitterly at the loss of his kind-hearted protector, was consigned to the care of his uncle Abu Talib, the second of Abd Al-Muttalib's five surviving sons. Az-Zubeir, the eldest, inherited the official duties of his deceased father; but he soon passed that honor on to the fourth son, Al-Abbas, a money-lender, owner of Zemzem, rich, but unfortunately weak in character. Abu Lahab, the third son, was destined to be a life-long foe of the Prophet; but the youngest, Hamza the hunter, was from the beginning one of his staunchest supporters. Abu Talib, a dealer in cloths and perfumes, was a poor man, yet he faithfully cared for his nephew, whom he almost never let out of his sight. When Mohammed was twelve, he accompanied Abu Talib on a mercantile journey to Syria; and various writers have mused at length on the probable effects of this strange, wild expedition on his highly susceptible mind. It may be, as some believe, that the seeds of his heavenly mission were sown in his mind during this experience. Whatever else he was, however, Mohammed was not a youthful prodigy, and perhaps, as most lads of his age would have done, he merely had a good time.

III

While Mohammed's life glided from youth into manhood without many remarkable changes, certain events occurred that indelibly fixed the channels of his future. The death of Abd Al-Muttalib had left the ancient house of Hashim without a strong leader, and so it happened that another branch of the Koreish came into power—a circumstance that marked the beginning of the deadly struggle between the Prophet and many of his kin that attended his whole career. For some years, it is true, this hostility was latent. During a decade—from Mohammed's tenth to his twentieth year—all the Koreish were banded together against the hostile tribe of the Beni Hawazin in the Sacrilegious War: a struggle that grew out of a violation of the taboo on fighting during the sacred months. When Mohammed was nearly twenty, he accompanied his uncles during one of the many frays that marked this civil strife; but his activities seem to have been confined to picking up the arrows of the enemy and turning them over for the use of his uncles. Many years later he remarked: "I remember being present with my uncles in the Sacrilegious War; I discharged arrows at the enemy, and I do not regret it." But the Prophet of divinity was always very human, and it seems almost certain that the enormous prestige of his station induced him occasionally to indulge in a verbal license pardonable in prophets if not in lesser men. With a wisdom that has characterized certain other heroes of divinity, Mohammed wisely confined his originality and his daring strictly to his mental activities, and fought only when self-preservation necessitated it.

The war finally ended in an unsatisfactory truce: neither side had won, and no dominant personality had yet emerged from the Koreish. Factionalism soon grew to be so rife that the descendants of Hashim, and families of germane origin, formed a confederacy to punish wrongdoing and secure justice among the different branches of the Koreish. Mohammed himself was an interested spectator of the initial ceremonies of this brotherhood. "I would not exchange for the choicest camel in all Arabia," he exclaimed on a later day, "the remembrance of being present at the oath which we took in the house of Abdallah when the Beni Hashim, Zuhra ibn Kilab, and Teim ibn Murra swore that they would stand by the oppressed." Thus, by slow degrees, the breach widened between Mohammed and the majority of the Koreish.

His early manhood was spent in caring for flocks, in attending caravan expeditions, and in certain avocations which, all things considered, indicated that he was more estimable than the common run of youthful Arabs. As a shepherd of sheep and goats on the hills around Mecca, he both conferred benefit upon his penurious uncle, Abu Talib, and engaged in an occupation that, as he was careful to point out on a future occasion, was particularly appropriate for his rank. After commenting on the similarity between himself and Moses, David, Jesus, and other seers, he concluded thus: "Verily there hath been no prophet raised up, who performed not the work of a shepherd." He often accompanied caravans, traveling possibly as far as Egypt and the Dead Sea. In addition to the money thus earned, he picked up a mass of miscellaneous information that he used both to his advantage and disadvantage in the Koran; for its pages reek with foreign phrases, now beautiful and now outrageously grotesque, which even his most intimate friends failed to comprehend. All writers, including strangely enough those of the Christian faith, coincide in stating that his early manhood was marked by an excess of modesty and a minimum of vice rare, not merely in young Arabs, but in the young men of any nation. It has been maintained, with a cogency no less admirable than indemonstrable, that his virtue was miraculously kept immaculate. Mohammed himself, with forgivable modesty, appears to have believed this. "I was engaged one night feeding the flocks in company with a lad of Koreish," he once narrated, "and I said to him, 'If thou wilt look after my flock, I will go into Mecca and divert myself there, even as youths are wont by night to divert themselves.'" But the sequel, though divinely ordained, was rather tame. As he neared the outskirts of the city, a marriage feast attracted so much of his time that he fell safely asleep. Another evening, as he approached the city bent upon a similar enterprise, strains of celestially somnolent music made him fall into a second scatheless slumber. "After this I sought no more after vice," he affirmed; but he thought it wise to add the cryptic phrase, "even until I had attained unto the prophetic office."

By the time Mohammed was twenty-five, Abu Talib, whose waxing family was constantly restricting his already limited means, decided that it was high time for his dependent nephew to shift for himself. "I am, as thou knowest, a man of small substance," he remarked one day to Mohammed, "and truly the times deal hardly with me. Now here is a caravan of thine own tribe about to start for Syria, and Khadija, daughter of Khuweilid, needeth men of our tribe to send forth with her merchandise. If thou wert to offer thyself, she would readily accept thy services." The double-edged nature of the conclusion presumably escaped both men; but the complaisant Mohammed acceded and was soon off on the journey, accompanied by Meisara, the servant of Khadija. Mohammed had thus far had little business experience, but he always showed a many-sided talent for barter and compromise, and he therefore returned with a credit that did him high honor. As the caravan approached Mecca, Meisara induced him to carry the good news to Khadija in person. That lady, a wealthy widow of about forty and the mother of three children, was highly elated at Mohammed's story; and, as she listened to the proof of his business ability and fondly scanned his large, nobly formed head, his curling, coal-black hair, his dark, piercing eyes, and his comely form, it naturally occurred to her that this vigorous and handsome young fellow would make an excellent successor to her deceased husband. She had turned down the proposals of many vehement Koreishite suitors; but here was one for whom, if necessary, she herself was prepared to do the wooing—for Arab ladies rarely entertained any foolish feminine scruples about such matters.

It was necessary; but she moved with discretion. She sent an envoy, probably Meisara, to find out why Mohammed was so timid about matrimony; for most Arabs married at about eighteen and lived in poverty ever after. "What is it, O Mohammed, that hindereth thee from marriage?" queried the messenger. "I have nothing in my hands wherewithal I might marry," he replied; for he still retained painful memories of a proposal refused by one of his cousins, on the sensible grounds that he had not the proper means to support her. "But if haply that difficulty were removed," he was asked, "and thou wert invited to espouse a beautiful and wealthy lady of noble birth, who would place thee in affluence, wouldst thou not desire to have her?" "But who might it be?" he quickly inquired. "It is Khadija." "But how can I attain unto her?" "Let that be my care," he was told, and he immediately responded, "I am ready."

Khadija was overjoyed at this news; but, according to custom, she still had to win the consent of her father despite her age and her manifold attainments. So she prepared a feast and made him drunk; she then commanded that a cow should be killed, and, drenching her intoxicated parent in perfumes, she clothed him in the requisite matrimonial robes. Under such circumstances the old man unconsciously performed the ceremony, but when he recovered he looked with amazement on all the numerous signs of a wedding, and stupidly inquired what it all meant. Upon learning the facts, and upon being misinformed to the effect that "the nuptial dress was put upon thee by Mohammed, thy son-in-law," he staggered up in high wrath and swore that his daughter, whose hand had been sought by the most eminent Koreishites, should never be the bride of such a shiftless ne'er-do-well as Mohammed. Even after the story had been corrected he still refused to relent, and a tribal war might have followed had he not shortly calmed down and decided to make the best of a bad job. During the next fifteen years Mohammed led a tranquil life. His future was provided for; he had plenty of leisure to occupy himself as he chose, for Khadija insisted upon running her own business affairs; and, notwithstanding her seasoned maturity, there seems to be little reasonable doubt that he became the father of four daughters and an indeterminate number of sons.

Not wishing to remain entirely idle, however, he acquired a partner and established a general barter and trade business in Mecca—a fact that doubtless explains the frequent depiction of Allah as a divine bookkeeper in the Koran: "God is good at accounts," and so on. Years later, in the heyday of his fame at Medina, he still bought goods wholesale and retailed them at an excellent profit, and he also employed his stentorian voice as an auctioneer. All his children turned out to be sickly. His son, or sons, died in infancy, and his oldest daughter lived less than forty years; hence historians who possess a flair for matters pertaining to medicine have made the deduction that perhaps, after all, his youthful zest was not guarded by Heaven, but was expended in most deplorable channels. During these years Mohammed and his wife continued to be conventional idolators who performed nightly rites in honor of various gods and goddesses—among whom Allah and his female consoler Al-Lat ranked fairly high—and who gave Pagan names to their children. And so, by the year 610, Mohammed at forty was nothing more than a respectable but unknown tradesman who had experienced no extraordinary crisis, whose few extant sayings were flat and insipid, and whose life seemed destined to remain as insignificant and unsung as that of any other Arab.

III

ALLAH AND MOHAMMED

I

The steps by which Mohammed emerged from obscurity into the full glow of his messianic mission can never be traced with any certainty. Explanations and interpretations in plenty—economic, rationalistic, psychological, mediumistic, and so on—have too often been advanced with placid and perfect assurance; but unfortunately they have not overcome the main difficulty: Mohammed himself. The enigma of his character—a fusion of the furthest limits of charlatanism, demagoguery, bombastic egotism, and general intellectual incompetency, with the opposite extremes of willing martyrdom, unaffected simplicity and sincerity, and lightning flashes of divine poetry—still remains essentially unchallenged and intact. He used tricks common to fakirs—was he therefore a complete and unabashed fakir? He began as a humble religious leader, and he ended as an adroit politician and powerful general—was he therefore dishonest from the start? He hid himself during battles—was he therefore always a coward? He often broke faith with friend and foe alike—was he therefore utterly unscrupulous? And yet

. . . He quite certainly believed in the divinity of his mission—was he therefore wholly sincere? He wrote some passages almost incomparable in their emotional beauty—was he therefore inspired? He kept Allah in the foreground while he himself remained in the background—why, then, did the influence of Allah wane as the prestige of Mohammed waxed? In short, was he a vicious paranoiac who developed into a maniacal monster, or an unrivaled genius who was all that his worshipers claimed—or both?

Such interrogations face the tracker of Mohammed's career at every turn of the journey, and, in avoiding the pitfalls on one side, he is very likely to stumble into the abysses on the other. For the facts of his life are at once too abundant and too few; and he who ponders them is ever apt to discover that, just at the moment when he confidently believes he is on the right path, he knows both too much and too little. The rainbow's end is forever at hand and yet forever distant; and similarly the intangible, chameleon-like personality of Mohammed constantly eludes and mocks one at the precise time when one is most confident of touching and cornering the flitting phantom. Under the circumstances, a rapid recapitulation of such concrete events as have been handed down with a minimum of bias is perhaps least likely to lead one too far astray.

II

When Mohammed was about thirty-five, the holy Kaba, beaten and broken by a violent flood, was in sad need of repair. A Grecian ship, that had been providentially wrecked on the coast of the Red Sea near by, furnished the materials necessary for its reconstruction. So great was the reverence emanating from the sacred walls, however, that the Koreish feared the imposition of heavenly wrath on those who made bold to tear the building down; but one fellow, braver than the rest, raised an apologetic prayer to Allah and simultaneously struck a heavy blow with a pickaxe. All those present, including the assaulter, then fled and lingered timorously until morning, when the incredible fact was noted that Allah had not spoken one way or the other, and so the structure was rapidly demolished. All went well with the building operations until the time came to replace the Black Stone in the eastern corner—an honor so great that each branch of the Koreish contended for it, until bloodshed was imminent. Finally the eldest patriarch in the city arose and advanced this ingenious solution: "O Koreish, hearken unto me! My advice is that the man who chanceth first to enter the court of the Kaba by yonder gate, he shall be chosen either to decide the difference amongst you, or himself to place the stone." Universal applause followed and everyone waited to learn who should be the lucky man. Just at this moment the unostentatious yet dignified form of Mohammed was seen to approach, and all the people shouted in unison: "Here comes the faithful arbiter; we are content to abide by his decision." Mohammed, ever cool and composed in public, calmly accepted the appointment and immediately devised a supremely clever diplomatic scheme that would certainly be satisfactory to all. He removed his cloak and laid it on the ground; then, putting the awful stone on it, he said: "Now let one from each of your four divisions come forward, and raise a corner of this mantle." This was done and, when the rock was level with the cavity, he himself thrust it in position. Thus the unpretentious tradesman rose in the twinkling of an eye to high eminence in the esteem of his townsmen. Since Mohammed's mind always took to omens and auguries as a duck takes to water, it is possible that this occurrence marked the vague inception of his mission.

At all events, about five years later his neighbors became much mystified by his behavior. He would retire, for days at a stretch, to a cave in the foothills of Mount Hira, a conical hill several miles north of Mecca, whither Khadija too sometimes went with him. Meanwhile his business languished, and various conjectures were advanced to account for his odd conduct—was the fellow crazy, or afflicted with some loathsome disease, or was he perchance engaged in some such nefarious occupation as counterfeiting? As the months passed, he still continued to act in the same incomprehensible manner, and it was noticed that, little by little, certain members of his immediate family attended him to his refuge, or gathered with him in some one of their own houses. This sort of thing went on for several years, until it was noised abroad that the quondam merchant and camel-driver was confidently claiming the honor of having made the epochal discovery which he phrased thus: *"La ilaha illa Allah, Mohammed rasul Allah"*—which, freely interpreted, means: "There is no god but Allah, and Mohammed is His Prophet."

This brief, twofold credo demands considerable attention. The first postulate was not entirely new, for Allah had hitherto been a well-behaved deity Who was highly regarded by many Arabs; yet, after all, He had been but one of many idols. By what process of thought had Mohammed come to exalt Allah not merely above all Arabian gods, but above the gods of all time? and furthermore, why was he so certain of his own intimate association with Allah?

Various explanations were offered by his simple-minded followers. According to one account, as Mohammed was wandering near the cave, "an angel from the sky cried to him, 'O Mohammed, I am Gabriel!' He was terrified, for as often as he raised his head, there was the apparition of the angel. He hurried home to tell his wife. 'O Khadija,' he said, 'I have never abhorred anything as I do these idols and soothsayers; and now verily I fear lest I should become a soothsayer myself.' 'Never,' replied his faithful wife, 'the Lord will never suffer it thus to be.' " So she made haste to get the opinion of her own relative, the aged visionary Waraka, who, after listening attentively to her tale, cried aloud: "By the Lord he speaketh truth! Doubtless it is the beginning of prophecy, and there shall come upon him the *Great Namus,* like as it came upon Moses." According to another story that is even more edifying, Khadija discreetly tested the genuineness of the angelic guest by making Mohammed sit first on her right knee, and then on her left; and the spirit did not object to either procedure. But when she took Mohammed in her lap and started to remove some of her garments, the virtuous apparition departed in great haste, and the crafty Khadija then exultantly cried: "Rejoice . . . for by the Lord! it is an angel, and no devil."

These enlightening tales, however, deserve to be supplemented by certain other considerations. Outside of

Arabia, Paganism was in general disrepute. The dissolute and declining Romans were cracking lewd jokes in the very faces of their gods; the myriad followers of Confucius, Buddha and Zoroaster were either too remote or too helpless to matter one way or another; Talmudic Judaism and Oriental Christianity despised idolatry and worshiped the same Jehovah, even though they disputed with each other, and indeed among themselves, concerning the various attributes, amorous pursuits, and lineal descendants of the Godhead. Now, to one who chose to regard himself as a prophet, monotheism had distinct advantages over polytheism. For one thing, it was rather confusing to attempt to obey the behests of conflicting deities; and for another, the different prophets of Jehovah in Judaism and Christendom had, so far as Mohammed knew, been uniformly successful—for he was familiar with the glorious history of Abraham, Moses and David, and he always held to the perverse belief that Jesus was not crucified. However deep in the dumps prophets may have been on occasion, they have invariably believed one thing: victory for their particular cause will inevitably come. Neither an unbroken series of worldly failures nor the chastisements of his God have ever shaken the faith of a first-class prophet in himself—or, as he would doubtless prefer to say, in his Divinity. Arabia—

broken, unorganized, inglorious, idolistic Arabia—obviously lacked one Supreme Being whose prerogative was greater than all other Supreme Beings; and that Being, in turn, needed a messenger to exploit His supremacy. The messengers who had served Jehovah had certainly prospered well; but Jehovah Himself appeared to be on the decline—His Unity was steadily disintegrating into a paradoxical Trinity. Why, therefore, not give Allah, perhaps the leading icon in Arabia, an opportunity? Such considerations quite probably never entered the head of Mohammed with any definiteness; yet his behavior for the rest of his days seems to indicate that these, or similar conceptions, were subconsciously egging him on.

Of certain facts, moreover, he was definitely aware. He may have had little or no formal education, but his memory was retentive and capacious, and his caravan journeys, together with the scores of conversations he had held at the yearly fairs, as well as at Mecca, with many cultivated strangers, had packed his mind with a mass of highly valuable if heterogeneous matter. In these ways he had learnt both the strength and the weakness of the Jews and Christians: their fanatical enthusiasms and despairs; their spasmodic attempts to proselytize as well as the widespread defections from their faiths; the loftiness of their moral and political codes—a loftiness that remained fruitless from their lack of cohesion and effectual leadership. Since his conception of religion was largely personal—for he looked upon Moses, Jesus and the rest merely as capable men who had founded and promulgated religions—and since Arabia had no preëminent ruler, why should *he* not seize the reins of power and carry on the great tradition of prophethood? What a magnificent opportunity beckoned, and how fortunate that he had been the first to recognize the call! By keeping only what was best in the Arabic faith—the Kaba and the Black Stone—and by a judicious selection of the most feasible ideas that lay imbedded in Jewish and Christian precepts, he might establish a code that would supersede all others, and might then dictate to all Arabs alike. What prophets had done, he would also do—and do better. Furthermore, he knew something else: he had a wealthy wife and four intimates who were already prepared to fight for him to the death.

Khadija rated first. From the beginning she had stood faithfully by his side, and whenever he was low-spirited and his heavenly visitations were temporarily suspended, she would tenderly comfort him—for the sad memories of her first marriage had made her determined that her second husband should succeed in whatever business he undertook. Her cousin, the learned mystic Waraka, readily abandoned his firm conviction that Christ was the only true prophet in favor of his cousin-in-law's exclusive claim to the same honor; and it is probable that he, more than any other person, enlightened Mohammed's many-sided ignorance of religious history. Mohammed had early adopted his youthful cousin Ali, son of Abu Talib, and the attachment between them had come to be mutually strong. He had also assumed control of Zeid, a Christian slave, who became so devoted to his master that, when he was offered his freedom, he replied: "I will not leave thee; thou art in the place to me of father and of mother." This pleased Mohammed so much that he immediately escorted Zeid to the Black Stone and said: "Bear testimony, all ye that are present. Zeid is my son; I will be his heir, and he shall be mine." In his thirty-ninth year Mohammed had become acquainted with Abu Bekr—commonly called either "the Sighing" or "the True"—a rich cloth merchant who was middle-aged and short, and who had deep-set eyes. Shrewd and penetrating in business concerns, mentally stable, and untroubled by too many disturbing ideas and emotions, he was just the sort of person Mohammed most needed: a devoted adherent who would serve as business agent for the new faith.

But in the beginning these were all. Some of his

immediate relatives did not take him very seriously: Abu Lahab grimaced in his face, and even the charitable Abu Talib smiled rather derisively at his curious actions. We are told that Abu Talib, chancing to apprehend his son Ali and Mohammed contorting themselves according to the precepts of Islam, thereupon remarked that he would not care to twist himself so that his middle portion would be higher than his head—a flippancy that Ali cherished and chuckled over years after his father's death. Meanwhile the great bulk of the Koreish were too contemptuously indifferent to pay any heed to Mohammed's strange yarnings, though occasionally, as he passed cliques of them on the streets, they would lazily point him out as a harmless and but mildly amusing dunce.

III

Without applauding or deprecating this Koreishite behavior, we may at any rate impartially consider its origin. The hitherto mentally and emotionally normal trader, husband and father had found himself suddenly swept off his feet and carried irresistibly away on a mighty tide: the perverse, inexplicable desire to write poetry—a fantasy that could not fail to make him the laughing-stock of all right-minded Meccans. How curious, how odd, that he, a well-to-do merchant who had looked forward to nothing more exciting than a peaceful and prosperous future, should be summarily wrenched from his moorings and cast adrift upon such a strange, tempest-tossed sea! Surely, surely, there was some marvelous meaning in the business—if he could but find it. And so, stabbed by agonizing doubts or transported with rapturous ecstasies, he plunged blindly on, seeking relief from his vague imaginings in intermittent bursts of formless, rhapsodical verse. His perturbed spirit now soared to the heights of Heaven and now plunged into the chasms of Hell; moments of ethereal bliss would be followed by periods of the profoundest melancholy. In short, he was passing through the throes of an experience closely akin to religious conversion—an experience that can end in but one of three ways: in a relapse into sin, in suicide, or in a more or less enduring catharsis of the spirit. Though Mohammed was too strong a man to return to the fleshpots of Arabia—if, indeed, he had ever tasted them—it is almost certain, as the earliest fragments of the Koran hint, that he meditated self-destruction for a time; but Allah, the All-Compelling, the Mighty One, had other plans.

It is related that the angel Gabriel, who thus far had labored only in the field of Christian employment, was chosen by Allah as bearer of the divine revelation to Mohammed. One day, while the trader-poet was wrestling with his doubts among the foothills of Mount Hira, he saw a wondrous apparition floating downward on celestial wing. Coming within a distance of two bowshots—for the Arabs are very accurate about such things—the divine envoy exposed a tablet covered with heavenly hieroglyphs before Mohammed's astonished eyes and exclaimed, "Read!" "I cannot read," replied Mohammed; but again the unearthly voice uttered the word, "Read!" And then, impelled by an irresistible power, Mohammed fixed his entranced eyes upon the document and began to chant thus:

> "Recite in the name of the Lord who created—
> Created Man from nought but congealed blood;—
> Recite! For thy Lord is beneficent . . ."

and so on, until the end. "Thou art God's Prophet, and I am Gabriel," announced the awe-inspiring guest before he departed to receive the blessing of Allah for having so successfully executed the heavenly command. Gabriel, in truth, was a very valuable ambassador, for, through the to and fro journeyings of this indefatigable messenger, Allah was able to remain at ease in Heaven, thus keeping up that appearance of intangible, majestic remoteness so necessary for dignified gods.

And thus Mohammed came into his own. From that moment he looked upon himself as Allah's vicegerent, through whom Allah's incontestable decrees were to be given to man—although Gabriel, or the Holy Ghost (for Mohammed's slipshod knowledge of Christian theogony led him into the regrettable error of perpetually confusing those two eminent divinities), continued in his capacity as interpreter of the intermittently revealed series of tablets. And so careful was Allah to eliminate the possibility of merely human invention that He prefaced every Sura, or individual revelation, with the express or implied injunction "SAY" or "SPEAK"—the irrefutable proof of divine authorship. Mohammed's every doubt had now vanished, his soul was completely at ease; and from his lips there burst the wildly exultant chant: *"La ilaha illa Allah, Mohammed rasul Allah!"*

Such, we may believe if we so desire, was the origin of the Koran, of Mohammed the Prophet, and of Islam itself—those three interacting and inseparable forces (a sort of Pagan Trinity, in fact) which, emerging when Rome was dying and Christianity was barely out of its cradle, convulsed the civilized and uncivilized world for centuries to come. Inasmuch, however, as Mohammed himself, not to mention his commentators, has added certain clarifying details that were touched with an earthiness foreign to the pretty picture, it may not be wholly presumptuous or irreverent to glance briefly at the other side of the canvas.

The conception of a flexible revelation—of one that could be indefinitely extended, amended, expurgated, or even abrogated in part—was excellent in many ways. Christianity and Mormonism, to cite only two counter cases, have both suffered somewhat, perhaps, from the inexorable nature of their scriptures. Woe unto him who alters a jot or tittle of their contents! At the same time, the precise meaning of the Christian creed, in particular, is very indefinite; it permits a latitude of interpretation, even in fundamental matters, that has brought about those lamentable schisms into major, minor and microscopic sects with which everyone is familiar. But, however much civil strife Islam may have endured from political factionalism or antagonism over inconsequential tenets in the Koran, it has remained indissolubly firm in its adherence to its supereminent divinities: Allah and Mohammed. And the credit for this, it is to be suspected, is due principally to the one whom all orthodox Moslems believe—or profess they believe—to be the lesser.

Poetry and oratory—the only forms of literature known to the Arabs—were both oracular and rudely rhythmical; and Mohammed, who from his childhood had been familiar with the yearly contests of poets and orators at the fairs, naturally adopted a cognate medium of expression. His thoughts, whether conceived in a white heat of frenzy or with deliberate coolness and sly calculation for the main chance, were probably not written down in any definite way during his life. It is not certain, in fact, that he could either read or write. He delighted in the appellation "the illiterate Prophet," possibly on account of his humility, and possibly because he knew that inspired ignorance had been the indisputable prerogative of all successful prophets in the past. Indeed, the very fact that he was unlearned was rightly supposed to increase the miraculous nature of his revelations. As he tossed the divine emanations from his lips, they were sometimes recorded by hired or willing scribes upon palm leaves, leather, stones, the shoulder-blades or ribs of camels and goats, or were even tattooed upon the breasts of men. But often they were not immediately written down at all; the Prophet would go around spouting them forth to his followers who, trained from infancy to memorize verses and songs of every sort with infallible precision, would piously commit them to memory. As a result of this divinely haphazard procedure, the time of composition of the different Suras has never been definitely fixed. Two facts, however, are well established: the revelations, at first very short, steadily increased in length; and, doubtless for that reason, the interminable later Suras do not even contain ashes—for ashes prove that flame was once present—whereas the earlier songs are occasionally touched with fire.

Occasionally . . . but only so. The indefeasible privilege of all Holy Writ to be dull—a privilege only too generously exercised—is abused in the Koran with an enthusiasm matched only by the third party of the Pentateuch. The spasmodic structure of the Koran—its absence of cohesion between chapters and even between sentences, its dithyrambic convulsions, its hodgepodge of inchoate and irrelevant ideas, its pervasive lack of charm—may be due, it has been hazarded, to Mohammed's neurotic idiosyncrasy; yet epileptic men of genius in many branches of mental activity have been by no means uncommon, and it seems simpler to assume that he was not born to be a poet. In any case, it is certain that his predilection for non-didactic poetry showed itself only at rare intervals: perhaps because, as the Koran puts it, "We have not taught him poetry, nor is it meet for him," perhaps because he had had no genuine love-affair in his youth, and perhaps because he believed that his commission was too serious to allow any protracted indulgence in such a frivolous thing as verse. Like the Hebrew prophets, he was at his best when raining heavenly maledictions on his enemies; like them, too, he was at his worst when he used repetition as a substitute for ideas. But they at least had good stories, taken from a long and rich racial history, to redecorate as they saw fit, whereas Arabia had almost no history worth the telling; and so Mohammed was compelled to fall back on Hebrew literature to help him out. He did fall back—again and again, and yet again. Even if he could not read, it was easy to get the necessary material from friendly Jews in Mecca; but an unfortunate, though apparently disregarded, difficulty attended this procedure: different Jews would tell the same story in different ways. So it came about that, when the Prophet was hard pressed for material, he would use one version; again, when his clock of inspiration had run down or been left unwound, he would use another garbled rendition of the same narrative. While the story of Joseph was his favorite, his collection of trophies pillaged from Biblical folklore included the activities of Noah, Abraham, Moses, David and less important notables; at the same time, he was quite innocent of the common Christian complaint that he had plagiarized the Bible, inasmuch as he had never read it. Carlyle was certainly not a tepid admirer of Mohammed, but, when he read the Koran, even his Berserker rage for great men suffered a serious shock—a shock that might justly be criticized for the very thing it criticizes. "I must say," he confessed, "it is as toilsome reading as I ever undertook. A wearisome, confused jumble, crude, incondite; endless iterations, long-windedness, entanglement; most crude, incondite;—insupportable stupidity, in short! Nothing but a sense of duty would carry any European through the Koran." And indeed, so far as that volume is concerned, the European sense of duty has been very small.

But with Mohammed's acolytes the case has been wholly different. For from the beginning they believed in the Koran with an appallingly artless simplicity, at once noble and absurd. Through its instrumentality, Allah the Wise, the Only Wise, revealed his immutable decrees: to the good, the rewards of a Paradise that utterly beggared the Christian Heaven, and to the bad the punishments of a Hell that contained an infinity of such refined tortures of heat, and even of cold, as neither the most imaginatively gifted Jew nor Christian had yet conceived—for Dante was undreamed of. Mohammed of course properly approved of Allah's decisions and judgments, as an employee should rightly behave toward his employer; and he was especially fond of his superior's delight in describing Hell—

"I swear," he gravely announced one day, "that it is one of the most serious things."

The earlier part of the Koran, or "Recitation," is mostly concerned with these elemental and primitive things; only at a later day did Allah—or Mohammed? —deal separately with the many matters touching the growth of a definite code of religious, social and governmental precepts. When scoffers poked ridicule at the rather sloppy grammar and metre of the Koran, Mohammed did two things: in the first place, after brandishing the doom of an eternity of roaring flames over their heads, he challenged them to produce better verses than his—or Allah's?—own; and, in the second place, he incautiously prepared a loophole of escape by revealing, in Sura 69, the fact that the Koran was "not the word of a poet," but "a revelation from the Lord of the Worlds." This lofty gesture temporarily squelched his defamers, who promptly dug off with their tails between their legs; but its effect did not last long when they reflected how damaging an admission he had made. It may of course be readily granted that precepts concerned with daily washing, food, taxes, and so on, were not especially well adapted to rhythmical prose; but, after all, that was Allah's and Mohammed's lookout. Perhaps, indeed, the confession of non-poetical power was scarcely necessary; for the inexplicable man who, in the pristine freshness of poetic glow, could indite this terse stanza, instinct with brooding doom:

> "In the name of Allah, the Beneficent, the Merciful.
> Say: I seek refuge in the Lord of men,
> The King of men,
> The God of men,
> From the evil of the whisperings of the slinking devil,
> Who whispers into the hearts of men,
> From among the Jinn and the men,"

and who conceived the charming fantasy that the lengthened shadows of morning and evening are elongated in obeisance to Allah, was also capable many years later of concocting an effusion designed expressly to make his wives behave themselves.

IV

"A PROPHET IS NOT WITHOUT HONOR"

I

ISLAM, the doctrine of "resignation to God," was now started on its way; but mystery hovers over every stage of the journey. The various explanations that have been devised to account for its marvelously rapid development have commonly just enough plausibility to make them romantically misleading; for the charm of a half-truth lies in its Lethean amalgamation of realism and fancy: it displays neither the dulness of unadorned fact nor the superficiality of exotic fabrication. In recent times Mohammed and his era have inevitably been subjected to treatment according to principles derived from the "scientific method." Now, while it is unquestionably true that a large amount of invaluable information has been accumulated thus, it is also true that the excessive use of this method has given rise to some definite dangers—dangers that are all the more alluring and deceptive because they bear the stamp of contemporary approval. For one thing, its adherents often lack the ability to apply the principle to their own mental processes: they sometimes manifest a bias as essentially unscientific as the fervent prayer of the most benighted Moslem. For another thing, its devotees frequently dispute among themselves over the validity of its countless ramifications with an enthusiasm unexcelled by political fanatics; and, for still another thing, the method itself is as much a product of conditions peculiar to the so-called Modern World as Islamism was a logical excrescence of the deplorable Dark Ages.

Although Mohammed's parents died so early as to deprive the Freudians of the opportunity to dissect him in a manner compatible with the most cherished articles of their faith, other not wholly dissimilar schools of thought have not failed to wield their scalpels—oftentimes with very considerable effect. For example, those who look upon him as a largely self-conscious medium who was extraordinarily skillful and successful in employing the cabalistic devices used by mediums as a class, have much to warrant their belief. The evidence extant in support of this view, in fact, merits respect if not complete acceptance. For the whole business of Allah, and Gabriel, and the magical tablets —whose precious contents none but Mohammed might gaze upon, and he only at infrequent intervals—is, to say the least, very intriguing. The problem that fronts all mediums is this: how to produce their messages without arousing the suspicion that they themselves are the authors; and innumerable devices are used to attain this end. It has been suggested that the Prophet himself may have solved the problem by a subtly clever device —his known susceptibility to epileptic fits. Before giving vent to one of Allah's inditements, he would snore, cover himself with a blanket, and remain thus until, drenched with sweat, he emerged and gave his message. One traditional account runs thus: "He fell to the ground like an inebriate, or one overcome by sleep; and in the coldest day his forehead would be bedewed with large drops of perspiration. Even his she-camel, if he chanced to become inspired while mounted on her, would be affected by a wild excitement, sitting down and rising up, now planting her legs rigidly, then throwing them about as if they would be parted from her." In the earlier Koran, he is characterized as the "man in the blanket," or the "man who is wrapped up." For he fully appreciated the necessity of keeping his followers in a state of protracted mystification, and to that end he made use of many theatrical tricks. He would drum up a crowd with his ludicrous snortings and puffings until the resounding cry, "Inspiration hath descended on the Prophet!" assured him that he had a sufficiently large audience to warrant the ebullition of a new Sura. While in a room that was obviously empty, he declared that all the seats were occupied by angels; he cultivated a suave and benign expression; he flattered and astounded his adherents by telling them intimately personal facts about themselves which he had presumably acquired through private information; he took the most painstaking care of his person—painted his eyes and perfumed his entire body every day, wore his hair long and probably dyed it when it became gray, and there is reason to believe that he always wore a veil. Eventually, he so perfected his technique that he could throw a cataleptic fit and produce a message without any previous preparation. In the midst of a meal he would contort himself, disgorge a new injunction, and then calmly finish his dinner.

Nor does the case for the prosecution end here. The manner in which his early disciples were won and organized suggests that like principles were employed. In the beginning, Islam was a profoundly secret society, whose leader frowned upon publicity but encouraged furtive proselytizing on a great scale—a policy of action that turned out to be perfectly suited to the situation. For this privacy doubtless saved the cause from early obliteration, while at the same time it offered the romantic attraction of a Jekyll-and-Hyde existence to those who accepted Islam—a circumstance decidedly favorable to the growth of any surreptitious conclave; and, in addition, it gave Mohammed time to pick and choose his lieutenants with care, as well as to school himself in the lessons needed for ruling heterogeneous masses of men. While all this was going on, he himself remained aloof in august, inaccessible grandeur, for none could see him who was not already rabid with desire to prostrate himself at the Prophet's feet. Thus, in those clandestine gatherings held in the house of the convert Al-Arkam—a house afterward appropriately immortalized by the title "The House of Islam"—and in the febrile activity of Mohammed's plastic pupils, headed by the efficient Abu Bekr, is to be found the germ whence all Islam sprang.

This reasoning sounds very plausible until one reflects: after all, could it have been as simple as this? And then an inscrutable image looms in the mind—the grotesque, grand, preposterous and prodigious figure of Mohammed.

II

The secret séances in the House of Al-Arkam continued; a variety of converts began to pour in; and by the fourth year of his mission Mohammed dared to come boldly out into the open and proclaim that he was the anointed representative of Allah. His proselytes at first were mostly humble folk: slaves, women unable to achieve matrimony, unsuccessful business men, and others who, discontented with their lot, were either looking for excitement or willing to take any chance however desperate. Yet it is a curious fact that every devotee, except Abu Bekr, showed some aversion before whole-heartedly accepting the new faith: "I never invited any one to the faith who displayed not hesitation and perplexity, excepting only Abu Bekr," the Prophet himself admitted. The explanation may lie in the fact that each proselyte was expected to remain true through thick and thin; indeed, his life was forfeit if he apostatized—a stipulation that, even today, makes the conversion of a Moslem a very difficult task. Another possible explanation is this: the converts soon discovered that Islam was not merely a gospel of salvation through faith—an outstanding tenet of all great religions, because it makes a peculiar appeal to the intellectually slothful—but a gospel that demanded a vast amount of hard work. Mohammed, in fact, had much more in common with James than with Paul. For if he was a fanatic in emotional matters, his grosser intellectual endowments were characterized by an admirable coolness and a logical precision that often confounded his friends and his enemies alike—though it is recorded that an early convert, who was commissioned to take down one of the Prophet's divine ravings, decided to renounce

Islam when he observed that he was permitted to pen whatever he chose.

Each newcomer recognized his brothers by the greeting "Peace unto you," a password of which Mohammed was especially fond; and if it was dangerous for a time to speak the words openly, recognition was made sure by the adoption of a peculiar style of turban. The new sect was called Moslems, or "traitors"—an appellation that provoked much merriment among Mohammed's less serious-minded opponents. He showed a typical lack of humor in accepting the sobriquet, they remarked, but he was to be praised for making it an honorable term; for, while it usually meant one who surrendered his friends to their foes, it now signified one who yielded himself to God. The Koran, however, settled the matter by affirming that the title had been invented by no less an authority than Abraham himself.

While converts of every type were welcomed, preference was naturally shown for those who had either physical or social strength. For a time most of them came from the descendants or adherents of the house of Hashim, and so Mohammed, doubtless with the idea of strengthening the faith by breaking the strong family and tribal ties, set up brotherhoods between those who came from different sects. The largeness of his nature is shown by his readiness to make amends for any wrong he had committed. A blind man once interrupted him, while he was earnestly conversing with a prospective convert, with the request that the Koran should be read aloud; and the Prophet, incensed at the ill-timed interruption, snapped out a harsh refusal. But his heart soon smote him, and he made atonement for his error by pointing out in the Koran how unforgivable it was for him to welcome the rich and powerful while neglecting the poor and despised. The most valuable of the slave converts was the negro Bilal, "small in body, but weighty in faith," whom Mohammed himself extolled as "the first fruits of Abyssinia." Almost all of the first score of converts remained staunch, though one of them, Obeidallah, eventually weakened under the strokes of persecution, became a Christian, and died in that faith; but Mohammed avenged himself by marrying his widow.

By far the most important of the Meccan neophytes, except Khadija and Abu Bekr, were the Prophet's uncle Hamza—a mighty man in hunting, wine and war, whose valorous conduct won him the title "The Lion of God"—and Omar, a veritable Hercules. He had been a clever trader who once outwitted the assessor of customs by making his own camel swallow the gold it carried—and he then recovered the money by killing the camel. His most cherished avocations had been wine, wife-beating, coarse interference in delicate feminine matters, and bitter hatred of Islam. Informed one day —so the most plausible tradition of his conversion runs —that his own sister and brother-in-law had yielded to its seductions, he hastened to their house and greeted them with the brotherly salutation, "I hear that ye are renegades!" When they tried to argue with him, he violently kicked the man and wounded his sister in the face. These activities so completely restored his good humor that he asked to see the roll they had been reading. Having perused a part of one Sura, he exclaimed, "How excellent is this discourse, and gracious!" adding that he would like to meet Mohammed. So he went immediately to Al-Arkam's house, where the inmates, including even the redoubtable Hamza, drew back in alarm; but the Prophet boldly seized his skirt and sword-belt and asked, "How long, O Omar, wilt thou not refrain from persecuting, even until the Lord send some calamity upon thee?" The penitent Omar replied, "Verily, I testify that thou art the Prophet of God!" whereupon Mohammed raised the joyous shout: "Allahu Akbar! Great is the Lord!" So widespread was the Koreishite fear of Omar that from this moment the Moslems prayed openly in the city; and the happy Prophet continued to exult over his prize acquisition in this fashion: "If Satan were to meet Omar, he would get out of Omar's way," while one of his pet sayings was, "I, Abu Bekr, and Omar."

It seems probable that Mohammed at first offered his disciples no promise of earthly rewards, but seduced them by painting gorgeously graphic pictures of their eventual felicity in Paradise, as well as the utter discomfiture of their foes in Hell. The Koran of this period abounds with eloquent descriptions of both places. Paradise is represented as a haven bulging with sensuous delights of the most naïve and ephemeral sort. In fact, so much emphasis was put upon food and drink that a jolly Jew objected on the ground that such continual feasting must of necessity be followed by purgation; the Prophet, however, swore that it would not even be necessary to blow the nose in Paradise, since all bodily impurities would be carried off by a perspiration "as odiferous as musk." Furthermore, he soon added particular attractions that were far more captivating than mere gluttony, even though they still lacked the subtlety of philosophic appeal.

> "Verily for the Pious is a blissful abode;
> Gardens and Vineyards,
> And Damsels with swelling bosoms, of an equal age,
> And a full cup."

He continued to dilate on this theme, rhyming the heavenly benefactions in pairs; but when he tried to include the angelic young ladies in the divine catalogue, their number utterly ruined his rigid metrical scheme, and he was therefore compelled to expatiate on their charms in prose: "lovely large-eyed girls resembling pearls hidden in their shells, a reward for that which the faithful have wrought. . . . We have made them virgins, fascinating, of an equal age." While thus innocently occupied, the faithful were to be further entertained by peering over the celestial battlements and observing the tortures of the unbelievers, who would be vainly trying to quench their thirst by drinking boiling water. "This shall be your entertainment on the Day of reckoning!" promises the Koran.

"Wherefore one day the Faithful shall laugh the Unbelievers to
scorn,
Lying upon couches, they shall behold them in Hell."

Spiritual inducements of this sort, not to mention the mundane rewards soon to be offered to the pious and the swift earthly doom promised for backsliders, did not fail in their effect. And still, despite the accessions to Islam, the Prophet as late as 615 was subject to public insult. The rigorous ban on bloodshed within tribes saved him from serious personal danger, but he nevertheless endured some very scurrilous abuse; his enemies would throw offensive objects at his person, or on his hearth while he was cooking his simple meals. One day they tossed in the entrails of a goat, and Mohammed, putting the refuse on a stick, carried it to the door and shouted: "Ye children of Abd Menaf! What sort of good neighborhood is this?" While at his devotions near the window, he was at times forced to crouch beneath a projecting stone to escape the missiles of his foes. But the prestige of his old protector, Abu Talib, was still very strong and, despite his regrettable adherence to the ancient faith, he staunchly protected his incomprehensible nephew from the Koreish. Once, it is true, Abu Talib's patience was shaken, and he asked Mohammed not to cast upon him "a burden heavier than I can bear." The Prophet, perturbed by his uncle's apparent desertion and by the prospect of his own consequent loss of protection, burst out crying and started to leave the room. Then the aged ruler was so moved that he cried: "Son of my brother, come back! And now depart in peace! and say whatsoever thou wilt. For, by the Lord of the Kaba, I will not, in any wise, give thee up for ever."

III

Notwithstanding the ubiquitous respect for Abu Talib and the equally widespread fear of Omar and Hamza, the Koreishite hatred of Mohammed became steadily more menacing. The lowborn fakir-Prophet might be a person of despicable origin who mouthed a prodigious amount of insane drivel, but he had certainly succeeded in kicking up a highly exasperating rumpus. The devil of it was that the pernicious fellow so skillfully blended his own revelations with Arabic and Jewish traditions, whose validity nobody impugned, that the Koreish could not denounce the one without laying themselves open to the charge of reviling the other. He appeared to be wholly impervious, not to say sublimely indifferent, to the appeal of common sense; for when the Koreish charged that his Suras were either fabricated by himself or dictated by abler assistants, he would employ the most underhanded means to disprove the accusation. When they suggested that, inasmuch as he identified himself with the prophets of old, he ought to trot out a few miracles, he unwisely obliged them by declaring that the sky would fall upon their impenitent heads. He realized his mistake, however, when they promptly demanded that he should fix a date for the catastrophe; and he then cleverly extricated himself from his predicament by maintaining that his presence in the holy city had averted the disaster. But Mohammed had learnt his lesson, and thereafter he never tampered with miracles—a fact that, perhaps more than any other, indicates his superiority over preceding prophets.

The Koreish, however, had not yet finished with him, and, as they redoubled their assaults, he met them in various ways. When one of them affirmed that the Prophet was a crazy man—"One taught by others, a Madman!"—under the influence of the dreadful Jinn, he retaliated by accusing his accuser of being a bastard who could not write, who was head over heels in debt, and who furthermore deserved a thump on the nose. When they worsted him in debate, he first lost his temper and then announced that he had been divinely commanded not to argue with unbelievers—for often, as Mohammed preached to his followers or fulminated against his antagonists, his cheeks would blaze and his voice would become shrill, and on one occasion he is said to have thrown dust on the heads of his opponents. When another Koreishite accepted the Prophet's rash challenge to a poetic duel to test the excellence of the Koran, Mohammed could do nothing but squirm in discomfiture; but he amply avenged himself, after the battle of Bedr, by ordering the summary execution of the despicable poet. When they pointed out the many errors of fact that appeared in the Koran, and sneered at his assertion that the revelation was "in pure Arabic," Mohammed at first replied that Allah must know best —"He hath revealed it who knoweth that which is hidden in heaven and in earth: He is forgiving and merciful"—but, when he was informed that his answer, though doubtless inspired, was hardly to the point, he attempted to dazzle everybody by producing a new Sura that nobody, not even himself, could comprehend. For Mohammed invariably trusted in Suras rather than syllogisms, and wisely quoted no authority save Allah.

If, however, he was safe from direct assault, the more humble of his auxiliaries—the slaves, strangers and lower classes—who lacked the protection of family ties, were not so fortunate. They were apprehended, beaten and jailed, or exposed to the terrific heat of the sun. Under torments of this sort, some of them naturally recanted—a contingency that necessitated swift measures on the part of Allah. Mohammed, sincerely moved by their sufferings, announced that, even though they dissembled to escape torture, Allah was nevertheless All-Merciful and Forgiving if their hearts were right; and a Sura forthwith appeared that poured divine wrath on every backslider, "excepting him who is forcibly compelled thereto, his heart remaining steadfast in the faith." One day the Prophet met an adherent who was weeping from the anguish of his wounds, and asked what the trouble was. "Evil, O Prophet! They would not let me go until I had abused thee, and spoken well of their gods." "But how dost thou find thine own heart?" "Secure and steadfast in the faith." "Then if they repeat their cruelty, repeat thou also thy words," advised Mohammed. Yet, in spite of this heavenly leniency, incessant persecution continued to diminish his little band, and he therefore counselled those who were defenseless to take refuge in Abyssinia. Some of them did so, but still the odious oppression continued.

The Prophet, in this desperate strait, seems to have resolved upon a desperate remedy. It is at all events true that, scarcely three months after the departure of the little company of refugees, he tried to effect a compromise with his implacable foes. Approaching a group of the Koreish in Mecca one day, he reeled off a Sura which contained the flattering information that some of their gods, and particularly their goddesses, were not so bad after all. Having enumerated several of them, he intoned this passage:

> "These are exalted Females,
> Whose intercession verily is to be sought after."

At the end of this strange encounter, Mohammed and his hearers promptly prostrated themselves and worshiped their individually pampered deities in a spirit of beautiful brotherhood.

This event probably marks the decadence of the mystic and the inception of the statesmanlike elements in Mohammed's character; but it was destined to bear bitter fruit. Had his co-workers possessed his aptitude for mental prestidigitation, all might have gone well; but, like others of his profession, Mohammed had stirred up a bigger hornets' nest than he realized. It appears that many Moslems, including even those who had been bribed into accepting Islam, actually believed that the Prophet had meant what he said about Allah, and himself, and Islam in general. Whatever it was that had inspired his retrograde action, Mohammed turned right-about-face in double-quick time; for another Sura followed posthaste, which declared that the Prophet, being very human, was sometimes deceived by the poisonous whisperings of the devil. It was furthermore stated that Allah, the Omnipotent, naturally possessed the power to erase or substitute sections of the Koran as he desired: "And when We change one verse in place of another (and God best knoweth that which He revealeth) they say, 'Verily thou plainly art a fabricator.' Nay! but the most of them understand not. Say, the Holy Spirit hath brought it down from thy Lord in truth, to stablish them that believe." Nevertheless, the clever device came to naught, for the Prophet's overplay of his hand led to two unfortunate results: the Koreish, more assured than ever that he was a slippery liar, redoubled their assaults on his devotees; and Mohammed himself was regarded with suspicious doubt by some of his most whole-hearted adherents.

Events followed thick and fast. The Prophet, disturbed and alarmed, advised another emigration to Abyssinia—a recommendation that swelled the rising fury of his enemies. For the Abyssinians, in years past, had invaded Arabia under Abraha, and what was more likely than that Mohammed was sending envoys to negotiate a *rapprochement* with their chiefs—a contingency that might foretell a second invasion to assist the Prophet and overthrow the Koreish? Impelled by such vague fears, they instituted a device far more effective than direct attack. Mohammed's biographers are not agreed upon the precise time when these events took place; but it seems probable that, shortly after the second emigration to Abyssinia (615–616), the Koreish issued a decree of excommunication against the family of Hashim—which meant practically all of Islam. Its descendants were banned from intermarriage or other business engagements with the Meccans; in brief, the Pagan bull specified that "dealings of every kind should cease." The effect was swift and inevitable—the relatively weak Hashimites were compelled to withdraw their forces from Mecca and retire to a secluded defile east of the city. And here for an indeterminate period running from several months to several years, the outlaws—probably about one hundred in number—lived as best they could by buying scanty provisions at fabulous prices from passing caravans. Mohammed's highly praiseworthy behavior under these desperate conditions restored, and indeed strengthened, the faith of the suffering Hashimites; it is even possible that, without this savage persecution, Islam might soon have died out and been forgotten in its infancy. For some of the better-class Moslems had heretofore been showing dangerous tendencies: they refused longer to kiss the Black Stone; they showed flagrant disrespect toward their unconverted relatives; they used obscene language; they even prayed to Allah while they were drunk; and—encouraged, alas! by the Prophet himself—they coveted the wives and possessions of the unbelievers. But this frightful ordeal cleansed their hearts of such wickednesses. The "blood of the martyrs" was, in all probability, the seed of Islam's glorious harvest.

And Mohammed himself was stirred to make even

greater efforts than ever. With the cries of starving children ringing in his ears, he would go forth, during the holy months when amnesty prevailed, to exhort the tribes that came to the fairs held at Ukaz and other places. "Ye people!" he would shout, "Say, there is no God but the Lord. Ye will be benefited thereby. Ye will gain the rule of Arabia and of foreign lands, and when ye die ye will reign as kings in Paradise." While he was thus engaged, his uncle, Abu Lahab (who had probably avoided the ban by forswearing his kinship to the tribe of Hashim), would tag after him, crying out, "Believe him not, he is a lying renegade!" On another occasion Abu Lahab yelled: "Blast the fellow! Is that all that he hath called us for together?" Mohammed was moved to such fury by this remark that he devoted one of the many imprecations of the Koran to his foul-mouthed, profligate uncle and his equally impenitent spouse.

> "Blasted be the hands of Abu Lahab; let himself perish;
> His wealth and his gains shall avail him not;
> Burned shall he be with the fiery flame,
> His wife shall be laden with firewood—
> On her neck a rope of palm fibre."

But Abu Lahab, who by fits and starts relied on the goddess Al-Uzza for protection, did not cease his mudslinging; and he was ably assisted by Pagans from foreign tribes who would taunt Mohammed thus: "Thine own kindred and people should know thee best; wherefore is it that they have cast thee off?" Then the Prophet would turn his face despairingly toward heaven and say, "O Lord, if Thou willedst, it would not be thus!" But Allah—Who, logically, should be as much of a nomad as his creatures—seems to have been enjoying a vacation just then.

In 619 the hostile edict was withdrawn; but the reasons for its abrogation are obscure. Some believe that the Koreish lifted it when (it must be repeated that the dates of these events are vague) Mohammed agreed to a compromise with the Pagan deities of Mecca; others think that the better nature of the Koreish at last caused them to pity the famishing exiles. Whatever the facts may be, it was discovered that the parchment on which the edict was written had been mostly devoured by some ants that, however, had taken devout care to leave the the inscribed name of God intact. The Koreish were so confounded by this direct manifestation of Allah's displeasure that, when five of their leaders declared they were opposed to the continued banishment of the Hashimites, opposition collapsed and the weary outcasts returned to their homes.

Mohammed, overjoyed at this unexpected good fortune and completely oblivious to the major part played by the insects, rightly gave thanks to Allah. But new, and even more sinister, events impended. Within a few months death deprived him of the loyal protection of Abu Talib and the tender ministrations of Khadija. He comforted his wife's dying hours with the assurance that she, together with three other well-known women —the Virgin Mary, Potiphar's wife, and "Kulthum, Moses' sister"—would occupy his chamber in Paradise; but all he could conscientiously promise his expiring uncle was that he would inhabit the coolest, or at any rate the least hot, regions in Hell. The contingent deaths of these two made the Prophet's position very precarious: Khadija had constantly nerved him to face the severest trials, and Abu Talib had just as constantly kept the number of those trials down. Abu Talib, in fact, was barely in his grave when the populace of Mecca cast dust on Mohammed's head; and he therefore betook himself to At-Taif, a city some seventy miles east of Mecca, to test its possibilities as a refuge. Arriving there early in 620, he was much disconcerted to learn that none of its inhabitants had even so much as heard of his ten-year-old mission; and when he attempted to enlighten them, the sheiks and their groundlings merely sneered in open contempt. He then besought them not to divulge his religious views—an exhibition of invaliant diplomacy that caused the people to hoot and hurl stones at him, until he fled from the city with blood flowing down his legs. Utterly cast down in spirit, he spent the next two months in seclusion at Mecca. During the pilgrimage month of Dhul-Hijja, while he was addressing the crowds of visitors in his usual way, a coincidence of measureless significance occurred. Mohammed chanced to notice a little group of men whom he recognized as inhabitants of Medina.

V

THE HEGIRA

I

Ancient Yathrib, commonly called Medina, was familiar to the Arabs as "the pleasing" city, for it lay in a fertile plain teeming with "green fields, running water, every blessing the Eastern mind can desire." For ages it had been inhabited by expatriated Jews; but early in the fourth century two Arab tribes, the Aus and the Khazraj, settled there. But the Hebrew residents were much superior to the newcomers in general culture, in agriculture and wealth, and, it was darkly rumored, in the black art of magic; for the Pagan usurpers held to the primitive belief that the perfect man was one who could write Arabic, swim and shoot —and not many of them could write Arabic. Jealousy of the more competent Jews, therefore, impelled the Yathribites to make war against them, and the sons of Abraham were decidedly disinclined to battle and bloodshed. Accordingly, having fought the Jews with very fair success, the two victorious clans had speedily decided to fight each other, with the result that Medina, for some generations, had been continually rent by tribal and civil wars. At present all parties were so tired of this everlasting strife that they had chosen one of the chief men among the Khazraj, Abdallah ibn Obei, to direct their fortunes; for the battle of Boath (616) had completely exhausted all the factions involved. Nevertheless, everybody was still dissatisfied, since it was feared that the truce was only temporary.

Now, for many centuries, despite one or two notable disappointments, the Jews had expectantly awaited the coming of a genuine prophet—a longing that had been communicated, probably through racial miscegenation, even to the Aus and the Khazraj—and lo! the news of Mohammed's ministry was already common knowledge at Medina. When the little troop of Medinese chanced to meet Mohammed at the sacred fair, therefore, they spoke thus with each other: "Know surely that this is the prophet with whom the Jews are ever threatening us; wherefore let us make haste and be the first to join him." For it was clear that languishing Medina, long disrupted by internecine struggles, needed above all else a leader capable of harmonizing all discordant elements and balancing the scales of justice impartially for all—except, it might be, the Jews—a leader, too, who would introduce no dangerous foreign ideas, but whose vital beliefs were grafted on a common Arabian stock. Perhaps there was some truth in the saying of Mohammed's child-wife, Ayesha, that the battle of Boath had been engineered by Allah for the benefit of the Moslems.

So, when the Prophet thus addressed the visitors, "Sit ye down for a little, and I will speak with you," they gladly obeyed. After he had explained the creed of Islam, with due emphasis upon his own part in it, he proceeded to narrate the dangers of his position at Mecca and next inquired what his prospects might be at Medina. They complimented him for his exalted rank, but expressed doubt as to his reception in their own embattled city. "If thou comest to us thus, we may be unable to rally round thee. Let us, we pray thee, return unto our people, if haply the Lord will create peace amongst us; and we will come back again to thee at this set time next year." So the men returned to Medina and quickly scattered the news of their marvelous encounter: would it not, they argued, be good business to claim the services of this very self-confident Messiah before he was appropriated by the waiting Jews, whose money-lending power held the mass of Yathribites in abject poverty?

This counsel appeared excellent to both the Aus and the Khazraj. After a year of troubled waiting on the part of Mohammed, his heart was gladdened at the sight of twelve men who arrived on the appointed day to welcome him as the anticipated saviour of Medina. This oath was then sworn to by all: "We will not worship any but the one God; we will not steal, neither will we commit adultery, nor kill our children; we will not slander in anywise; nor will we disobey the Prophet in anything that is right." Mohammed was so swept away by the general tone of obedience in this statement that he apparently failed to notice the joker in the concluding clause; and thus the First Pledge, or Pledge of Women—so called because its lack of martial ardor made it the only vow required of female Moslems—was made. The twelve apostles at once returned and the propagation of the new religion was soon in full swing. At the request of the Medinese, the Prophet sent one Musab—once a connoisseur of gaudy clothes and delicate perfumes, but now a ragged, rampant Moslem—to instruct them in the more intricate matters of Islam. So tremendous was the zeal for proselytizing that the most strenuous efforts were made to secure converts: the newly saved souls covenanted that they would not speak to anyone who did not acknowledge the Prophet, and all idols, as well as idol-worshipers, were treated with the utmost severity. The salvation of one old fellow, who habitually bowed before a horrid image in his house, was particularly affecting. Young devotees cast the idol into a noisome well every night; but every morning he just as regularly hauled up, cleansed it, and again went through his genuflections. One day, however, they hitched the vile thing to a dead dog before tossing it in the well, "whereupon he abandoned his image and believed." Before long new converts came in from every side with very little persuasion; for the Medinese were very human and, inasmuch as Islam was now all the rage, they wanted to be in the newest style.

While Medina was buzzing with these devout activities, Mohammed was otherwise occupied. Hemmed in by ever present dangers, and hearing only vague reports of the conflagration that was sweeping Medina, he was constantly on tiptoe with hopeful yet fearful expectation. If his body was still held at Mecca, his unbridled imagination was free to range toward the beloved north, where both Medina and Jerusalem lay; and one morning he astounded his townsmen by declaring that, during the preceding night, he had performed his devotions in the Temple of Solomon at Jerusalem. The obliging Gabriel, he said, had borne him on a winged steed over Medina to the Temple; the Arabian Pegasus, however, did not pause long there, but continued his celestial journey until he had carried his passengers completely out of this world, to those ethereal realms of bliss where the Seven Heavens lie. Up and still up they flew, while the Prophet carefully noted the order of precedence of those prophets whose model he had proclaimed himself to be: Jesus and John were in the second or third—he was not *quite* sure which—Moses was in the sixth, while Abraham alone had the supreme distinction of residing in the seventh. There, at the apex of indescribable glory, Mohammed had entered the awful presence of his Maker, Who, after some rather pointless chit-chat, charged him to see that all Moslems should hereafter prostrate themselves in prayer toward the Temple of Solomon five times every day. When Mohammed concluded, the Koreish laughed him to scorn, and even a few of the faithful were somewhat flabbergasted; but Abu Bekr saved the situation by declaring that he did not doubt the truth of this tale, inasmuch as he had already swallowed far more improbable yarns related by the Prophet. Yet the veracity of his amply substantiated narrative rests upon two solid facts: from that day to this, all devout Moslems have continued to bow themselves five times daily in prayer; and sceptics may still see, upon the rock where stands the Mosque of Omar in Jerusalem, the identical print of the Prophet's foot where he leaped upon the heavenly charger.

II

The year 621 glided peacefully away. Mohammed, occupied with thoughts of a glorious future at Medina, had lost interest in spreading the faith in Mecca; and the Koreish, deceived by his apparent inactivity, had largely ceased to trouble him. Musab eventually returned with a glowing account of the progress made at Medina; but the Prophet, whose caution was certainly no less pronounced than his courage, carefully guarded his enthusiasm until more definite proofs were at hand. They soon came. In March, 622, the date fixed for the second conclave, seventy-three Medinese came in obedience to the promise made in the preceding year.

This occasion was so profoundly important that Mohammed took an infinitude of pains to conceal it—even his trusted intimates did not know about it beforehand. The Prophet, accompanied only by his wealthy and trustworthy uncle Al-Abbas, met the delegates at dead of night in a secluded glen. Al-Abbas diplomatically broke the ice by stating that, while his wonderful nephew was happy, safe and contented in Mecca, he nevertheless preferred to establish himself at Medina—in case ample security for his safety were assured. To this harangue Al-Bara, leader of the visitors, replied:

"We have listened to thy words. Our resolution is unshaken. Our lives are at the Prophet's service. It is now for *him* to speak." Then Mohammed, beginning loftily as he always did by chanting long passages of the Koran, finally descended to the earth and informed them that he would be gracious enough to confer the boon of his presence upon Medina if its inhabitants would make an irrevocable vow to defend him, even as they would protect their nearest and dearest. A confused jargon of voices arose, eagerly assuring him that his person would be guarded at any cost. Al-Abbas, frightened almost out of his skin, breathed: "Hush! There may be spies abroad," and in low tones requested them to plight their faith. The chief replied, "Stretch out thy hand, O Mohammed!" He did so; and Al-Bara, followed by all the rest, struck his hand upon the Prophet's in token of fealty. This was called the Second Pledge, since it included an oath to fight for the Prophet, and the touching of his holy hand—an honor never given to the generality of women. The assembly then silently broke up.

Such a large body of men could not gather so close to Mecca, however, without rumors leaking out. Next morning the mistrustful chiefs of the Koreish called upon the visitors and informed them that their presence warranted the suspicion that they were interfering in the politics of Mecca—an act that virtually amounted to a declaration of war. The Medinese did the only possible thing: they replied that the Koreish were wholly mistaken, and the slow-witted Meccans were ingenuous enough to believe them. But the clever Yathribites had barely departed in high glee when the Koreish learnt the facts, and set out upon a vain pursuit. Thus foiled, the enraged Koreish at once vented their spleen upon the believers, to whom the Prophet accordingly gave this command: "Depart unto Medina; for the Lord hath verily given unto you brethren in that city, and a home in which ye may find refuge." Early in April the migration commenced, in parties of twos and threes, while the baffled Koreish looked on in stupefied amazement; for the number of clans that were involved in the movement prevented any concerted hostilities, since no one had the right to interfere in private family matters. By force or guile, however, they succeeded in corrupting some of Mohammed's coadjutors who were weakest in faith or family ties; but the great body of Islam—now numbering probably close to two hundred souls—got safely away. A royal welcome awaited them, for the Medinese converts, flushed with their novel fanaticism, bestowed every imaginable honor upon the refugees—one zealot even went so far as to offer his guest one-half of his property, and also added a special bounty in the shape of one of his wives.

But Mohammed, together with his family and the household of Abu Bekr, still lingered. He informed Abu that "his time was not yet come; the Lord had not as yet given him the command to emigrate." Whether or no the Prophet's decision to tarry was determined on account of a genuine desire not to leave the burning ship before all the passengers were safe, or because he cannily awaited further proofs from the Medinese before trusting his skin to them, must forever remain a matter for indulgent speculation. But in the middle of June he received the fearful intelligence that the Koreish intended to visit him. Their purpose is uncertain. It has been surmised that they had decided to assassinate him—for if, like Cæsar, he were to be pierced with swords driven home by representatives of every tribe, his weak clan would have to be satisfied with blood-money instead of blood-vengeance—to imprison him, to ostracize him, or to do no man knows what. That Mohammed himself was not privy to their intentions is indicated by this passage from the Koran: "And call to mind when the Unbelievers plotted against thee, that they might detain thee, or slay thee, or expel thee. Yea, they plotted, but God plotted likewise.

And God is the best of plotters." Tradition states that Gabriel informed the Prophet of the malignant design; he at once told Ali to lie upon his bed, then went forth, and simultaneously greeted the evil-comers with a handful of dust and this excerpt from the Koran, "And We have covered them so that they shall not see." For, indeed, the best of plotters had wrapped Mohammed in a cloak of invisibility; he therefore escaped undetected while the murderous men lay in wait, thinking that the silent figure on the bed was the Prophet until the morning light apprised them of their sad error. It seems more likely, however, that Mohammed merely threw his deceptive red mantle over the recumbent Ali, and then slipped out of the back window to join the trembling Abu Bekr, who wept joyous tears now that his superior had at last decided to leave Mecca.

For the next three days, the two men lay in concealment in a neighboring cave, while the distracted Koreish feverishly sought everywhere for them. The house of Abu Bekr was searched, but when his daughter Asma was asked, "Where is thy father?" she innocently replied, "Truly, I know not where he is"—whereupon Abu Jahl, a ferocious and impudent fellow, "slapped her on the face with such force that one of her earrings dropped." Meanwhile the two outcasts lurked in the secrecy of the cave, across whose entrance, we are informed, a divinely commissioned spider wove a protecting web; yet legends are often more industrious than spiders. Abu Bekr would shake with fear and breathe the low whisper, "What if one were to look through the chink, and see us underneath his very feet?" to which the Prophet would boldly reply: "Think not thus, Abu Bekr! We are two, but God is in the midst a third." Yet Mohammed loved Abu "more than all the world; he held no one equal unto him," sang the poet Hassan; and the generally taciturn and morose Prophet, listening to the song, was pleased and laughed so heartily that he held his sides and his back teeth became visible. "Thou hast spoken truly, O Hassan!" he remarked after he had recovered his breath, "it is just as thou hast said."

After three days had passed without their detection, it seemed safe to speed toward Medina. The careful Abu Bekr had fetched a purse, bulging with thousands of gold pieces, as well as two of his best camels; and, probably on the night of June 20, they mounted the beasts—Mohammed taking care to choose the swifter one, Al-Kaswa—and started on the perilous journey. The two-hundred-odd miles that they must traverse extended over a parched, barren, inexpressibly desolate and mournful waste, where only such rugged trees as the tamarind and acacia could exist, where phantom mirages mocked the eye, and all nature was but a ribbed and menacing skeleton. They traveled chiefly at night, resting during the sweltering heat of the day and buying provisions from such scattered Bedouins as they chanced to encounter. Abu Bekr, who was well known to most of these desert dwellers, was frequently asked who his friend was, and he regularly made the answer, "A guide to lead me," while the diplomatic Prophet kept a strict silence.

At length, after eight days of doubt and deprivation, they came in sight of Medina; but the wary Mohammed had no intention of trusting himself to the city before he knew exactly how things lay. "Lead us," he said to the guide, "straight to the Beni Amr at Koba, and draw not yet nigh unto Medina." This overscrupulous vigilance turned out to be unnecessary, for rumors of his approach had set the city agog with delight; and every morning a band of converts and refugees had posted themselves on a hill to watch his arrival. On this morning one of them, catching sight of the travelers as they trudged toward Koba, raised the rapturous shout: "Ho! he has come! he whom we have been looking for has come!" The marvelous news flew from tongue to tongue, and everybody rushed forth to Koba to greet the majestic guest. Even the children cried out: "Here is the Prophet! He is come! He is come!" while a great crowd surged around him and made profound obeisance. Then Mohammed knew at last that he was safe among friends. He had escaped from Mecca, where the Koreishite swords might have altered the course of events for all time; but the otherwise dull and sluggish Middle Ages were fated to be infinitely enriched by the romantic contest between the Crescent and the Cross. "Ye people!" he courteously proclaimed, "show your joy by giving your neighbors the salutation of peace; send portions to the poor; bind close the ties of kinsmanship; and offer up your prayers whilst others sleep. Thus ye shall enter Paradise in peace."

III

To make the assurance of a safe entrance to Medina doubly sure, however, Mohammed lingered four days at Koba. Even then he took no dangerous chances, for he requested the Medinese descendants of his revered great-grandmother, the spouse of Hashim, to attend him into the city; and in the meantime he had slept only when some of his most trusted underlings kept watch. These super-precautions proved to be needless, for tribe after tribe came flocking forth to see which could outdo the other in paying reverence to him. On every hand rose the earnest request: "Alight here, O Prophet! We have abundance with us, means of defense and weapons and room. Abide with us!"—and many suppliants emphasized their requests by seizing the halter of Al-Kaswa. On this occasion Mohammed's superb political ability was again evidenced. He would show no favoritism, but, by means of a camel and an omen—both inexpressibly dear to every Arab's heart—he would choose his abode by supernatural means. To all these fervent ejaculations he replied: "The decision rests with the camel; make way for her; let her go free." So Al-Kaswa, unguided by rein, moved forward until she entered the eastern section of the city, where, seeing a few date-trees in an open court-yard, she quite naturally ambled toward their grateful shade and awkwardly sat down. And in this way was the site for the Mosque chosen—the famous Mosque where, for the remainder of his days, the Prophet dwelt, married, prayed, preached, emitted new revelations, planned his schemes of conquest, greeted his friends, and uttered maledictions against his foes; where, also, he sickened, died and was buried. Yet certain abominable sceptics have intimated that Mohammed knew beforehand that this particular spot was already hallowed as a place of prayer, and that the rein of Al-Kaswa's halter was not so very slack after all.

The Prophet at once negotiated to buy the sacred

site. Its owners wished to make him a present of it, but he would not stoop to accept it as a gift; accordingly, it was purchased with ten gold pieces from Abu Bekr's wallet. For seven months Mohammed lived in the lower story of an adjacent house, owned by Abu Eiyub, while the construction of the Mosque, with its adjoining apartments for himself, went on. His bodily wants were provided for by the citizens, who contended with each other for the honor of sending him the choicest viands they could procure. As might be expected, Abu Eiyub was exceedingly solicitous for the comfort and safety of his distinguished roomer. Once, when a water-pot was accidentally broken in the upper story, Abu and his wife quickly sopped up the water with their clothes, and then rushed down to Mohammed's apartment in great fear lest a drop or two might have defiled his garments. Meanwhile the building of the Mosque was pushed at full speed. The Prophet himself joined heartily in the work, thus stimulating all his helpers to increase their efforts, and united with them in their labor-lightening song:

> "O Lord! there is no joy but the joy of futurity.
> O Lord! have mercy upon the Citizens and the Refugees!"

All this led to a spirit of fellowship between these two classes, and, in order that the union might be made more firm, Mohammed, after first setting the example, paired off individuals in each. "Become brethren every two and two of you," he gently commanded, and it was done.

One danger, unforeseen even by the perspicacious Prophet, soon threatened the refugees. The climate of Mecca, while excessively hot, was dry and salubrious; but, though Medina's altitude was unusually great, her drainage paradoxically enough was very poor, and the noxious exhalations from her stagnant water, abetted by intense heat at day and intense cold at night, soon prostrated large numbers of the refugees with fever. This misfortune so dampened the enthusiasm of many that, in their frenzied delirium, they would moan out their desire to go home. When Mohammed heard of this, he looked upward and raised this prayer: "O Lord! make Medina dear unto us, even as Mecca, or even dearer. Bless its produce, and banish far from it the pestilence!" But, for some inscrutable reason, Allah, the Hearer and the Answerer of Prayer, remained deaf for a time; and at one period Mohammed was one of the very few persons who were able to stand during prayers. When, however, he informed the recumbent invalids that "the prayer of one who sits is worth only half the prayer of him that stands," they all made desperate efforts to rise.

Nevertheless, the first few months at Medina were on the whole happy and auspicious. The elements of disaffection that lurked among the Jews and the unbelievers bided their day; the refugees and the citizen converts, or allies, gladly rushed to fulfill the smallest desire of the Prophet, whose fascinating personality completely charmed his friends and even intrigued his enemies—for a time. Who could resist the appeal of a man who gracefully bestowed names of good omen upon converts previously burdened with inauspicious Pagan titles, and who dignified those of his subordinates who were enslaved in the ignoble calling of "hucksters" by altering the forbidding word to "Merchants"? In an excess of praiseworthy devotion, they quaffed the sacred water in which the Prophet had bathed, and piously treasured his hairs and nail-parings as charms and forget-me-nots. And Mohammed, ever extraordinarily swift to take hints, soon formed the habit of wrapping up these personal relics and bestowing them upon new converts as a peculiar evidence of his esteem.

While his worshipers thus fawned and his foes maintained an ominously quiet peace, the Prophet calmly assumed the attributes of a sovereign and sacerdotal office. As self-appointed ruler of the city, he exercised the right of deposing and selecting whatever chiefs he desired; as priestly dictator of all Islam, he established those multitudinous rules and ordinances that still defy the assaults of time. Motivated probably by a statesmanlike, if rather cautious, wish to win or at least placate the Jews, he inaugurated a complicated system of devotion based principally upon the famous precepts that had been given to Moses. The detractors of Islam have so exaggerated its largely fictitious sensuality that its rigorous rites have too often been forgotten: its lustrations, its fastings, its prodigality of genuflections. The business of lustration, for example, was very complicated. Before prayer the Moslem must wash his face from the top of the forehead to the chin and sideways as far as both ears, bathe his arms and hands as far as the elbows, and cleanse his feet as far as the ankles; and all this must be done in the strictest silence, broken only by such prayers as the votary might think appropriate. While scrubbing his teeth, he might say if he chose: "Vouchsafe, O Lord, as I clean my teeth, to purify me from my faults, and accept my homage, O Lord! May the purity of my teeth be for me a pledge of the whiteness of my face at the Day of Judgment." If, through a momentary lapse into sin, the hapless believer had defiled his body, he thus washed away his iniquity: three successive times he poured water upon his right and left shoulders, and a like number of times on the top of his head; and should one hair on the entire body be left untouched, the act of purification was wholly vain.

The Prophet also instituted various fasts which, with certain alterations, have also endured. These fasts were, if possible, even more laboriously meticulous than lustration. While abstaining from food and drink, the Moslems must take the most scrupulous precaution to see that absolutely nothing entered the body. If they smelled perfumes, bathed, or carelessly swallowed their spittle, the fast was broken; the most ardent disciples would not even open their mouths to converse, for fear of inhaling too much air; and, if a thoughtless faster allowed a particle of food, no matter how small, to become wedged between his teeth, he was deemed to be a backslider from the faith.

December was for a time annually sanctified by fasting, and several rather diverting details followed. In the first place, most of the Moslems took the responsibility with such complete and abject seriousness that they unintentionally disturbed the Prophet's slumbers. Very late one evening they came to the Mosque for the service of prayer; and, observing that Mohammed was not on hand, they approached his house and coughed loudly before the door. The Prophet, now thoroughly aroused, came forth and addressed them thus: "I have observed for some days your coming for the nightly prayer at the Mosque, until I feared that it would grow by custom into a binding ordinance. . . . Wherefore, pray ye at eventide in your houses." He then returned to resume his interrupted repose; but a further trouble awaited him. His humble supporters, it appeared, were obsessed with the monkish idea that they should abstain from every conceivable pleasure during the whole month; but Mohammed was too wise to permit such immoderate asceticism. Allah, it was soon revealed, "willeth not for you that which is difficult. . . . It is lawful unto you, during the nights of the Fast, to consort with your wives. Now, therefore, sleep with them, and earnestly desire that which God hath ordained for you; and eat and drink until ye can distinguish a white thread from a black thread, by the daybreak. Then keep the fast again until night. . . . Thus God declareth His signs unto mankind, that they may follow Piety." The consequent popularity of the fast, indeed, brought new adherents to Islam in great abundance, until an unforeseen contingency arose. Abstinence from food and drink during the short days of December caused little difficulty; but the Prophet, trusting in that quaint omniscience which universally attends the assumption of prophetic robes, introduced an intercalary system based upon the lunar months.

The sacred month, therefore, gradually shifted from winter to summer, when the sixteen-hour days made what had previously been a pleasure a great burden; nevertheless, Mohammed persevered in his oddity, for to have done otherwise would have impugned his infallibility. So his faithful zealots groaned and were troubled, and longingly anticipated the new moon, when the fast was joyously broken by the bestowal of alms upon the poor and the resumption of normal bodily activities.

Five times a day the believers, no matter how pleasantly occupied, must turn to prayer: at dawn, at midday, in the afternoon, at sunset, and at the coming of complete darkness. On six days these devotions could be performed anywhere, though preferably in congregation at the Mosque; but every Friday the Moslems, unless detained by extraordinary causes, were commanded to worship in a body at the Mosque. The ever efficient Gabriel informed Mohammed of Allah's desire that the time for each prayer should be announced by a crier, who must shout: "GREAT IS THE LORD! GREAT IS THE LORD! I bear witness that there is no God but the Lord: I bear witness that Mohammed is the Prophet of God. Come unto prayer: come unto salvation. God is great! God is great! There is no God but the Lord!" So Mohammed instructed his negro servant, Bilal, to be the public crier; and early every morning Bilal would clamber upon a high house and rouse the slumbering Moslems with these words, adding this salutary invention of his own: "Prayer is better than sleep! Prayer is better than sleep!" Then, climbing down from his lofty perch, he would approach Mohammed's door and shout: "To prayer, O Apostle of God! to salvation!"

At the special Friday service, the Prophet ascended the pulpit, gave a stereotyped salutation of peace, and then seated himself while Bilal shouted the stentorian summons to prayer. Descending from the pulpit, Mohammed then led the prayers; reascending, he delivered one or two exhortations. The assembly, fixing their rapt glances on his earnest gesticulations, would swallow every word and at the end join in a loud "Amen!" or something like it. When all was over, his mantle of striped material from Yemen, and his girdle of splendid Oman cloth, were carefully folded up and laid away until the next service. The pulpit itself was soon endowed with an awful sanctity. Disputes were settled at its base; and should anyone take a false oath in its presence, "even if the subject were as insignificant as a toothpick"—and toothpicks were not wholly unknown in Islam—he thereby doomed himself to eternal damnation. Before it had been built, Mohammed had supported himself during his sermons by leaning on a post —an object of which he grew so fond that, after it was no longer needed, he commanded it should be interred beneath the pulpit. The post itself reciprocated his touching sentiment; for, when it was abandoned, it moaned loudly and would not stop until the Prophet placed his hand upon it, whereupon its grief was assuaged.

VI

HOLY WARS

I

THOUGH Mohammed was now actually the spiritual and nominally the temporal ruler of Medina, his position nevertheless was very precarious. The Jews, while completely deficient in martial valor, were openly contemptuous of his prophetical jurisdiction, and the Khazrajite leader, Abdallah ibn Obei, showed overt defiance against his assumption of civil power. Presumably because he feared and respected Abdallah's influence, the Prophet took pains to treat him with every courtesy; but the compliment was not returned. One day, when Mohammed chanced to observe his rival seated at ease in the cool shade of his house, he alighted from his steed, graciously saluted the sitter, recited some of the most affecting passages in the Koran, and finally invited him to adopt the faith. Abdallah listened composedly until the long harangue was ended; then he spoke. "Nothing could be better than this discourse of thine, if it were true. Now, therefore, do thou sit at home in thine own house, and whosoever cometh to thee preach thus unto him, and he that cometh not unto thee refrain from troubling him with that which he dislikes." He also casually mentioned the fact that he objected to the smell of the beast that Mohammed bestrode; so the Prophet went on his way, sorely stricken in spirit.

In other ways, too, he was equally unfortunate. His fabulous rise from the lowly state of an insignificant trader to the pinnacle of fame appears to have induced him to overestimate his powers; at any rate, soon after his arrival at Medina, he betrayed his ignorance of the simplest facts of Arabian agriculture by forbidding the artificial fecundation of palm trees, with the result that they became almost barren. But when his egregious error was pointed out, he manifested a wisdom rare in prophets by candidly admitting that he was in the wrong. "I am only mortal," he confessed. "If I give you an order in the domain of your religion then receive it; but if I give you an order from my own opinion then am I but mortal." In the near famine that had resulted from his bungling interference, there was poetic justice in the fact that he, as well as the rest, could eat only one date per day; yet he gladly shared in the stringent privations that all were forced to endure. While his own face was pinched with hunger, he divided with the most needy Moslems the gifts of food which various people had sent him; on one occasion he was glad to accept a Jew's offer to partake of a meal of rancid fat and barley bread; and for months, during the dead of winter, he went without any fire on his hearth.

It was obvious that such a state of affairs could not be permitted to continue. No matter how strong the already sorely tried faith of his partisans was, it would not forever withstand the shocks of rampant famine and naked, shivering misery; then too, and even more vital, was the consideration that new converts could never be won over to such a ragged and unkempt faith—Islam would not grow. And other even more subtle ideas were fermenting in Mohammed's ever restive mind. He, the one and only Prophet of the Most High Allah, was a starving outcast because of the pernicious activities of the overbearing, wealthy and rather cowardly Koreish, whose teeming caravans pursued their unmolested way northward from Mecca, between Medina and the Red Sea, to Syria. But the destitute refugees were pledged to advance the banners of Islam not merely in defensive, but, if Allah so willed, in offensive war; and should any of them see fit to remind him that, in earlier days, he had instructed them not to retaliate against their enemies, he could—and did—allay their squeamishness with a revelation. Furthermore, his henchmen had already been subjected, by chance or design, to a strenuous discipline that had inured them to endure such hardships as a career of pillage and guerrilla warfare would entail. Rigid religious fasts had accustomed them to withstand hunger and thirst; at the daily public *salat,* or prayer, they had been drilled to stand in rows, to perform what amounted to tough gymnastic exercises, and to expect celestial condemnation unless they scrupulously obeyed the minutest requirements of these incessant manœuvers. The successful plundering of opulent Koreishite caravans—which, under the circumstances, might reasonably be expected—would accomplish four excellent results: it would put a summary end to the ubiquitous suffering at Medina; it would provide a more than adequate outlet for the explosive zeal of his backers; it would conclusively demonstrate the prowess of Islam, thereby winning new members to the fold; and it would enable Mohammed to exult over the salutary discomfiture of his despicable foes.

How clearly defined these or other considerations may have been in the mind of the outstanding Oriental of the seventh century, it would be presumptuous for a twentieth century Occidental to say; the fact remains, however, that such were the results attained. Brahminism, Buddhism and Confucianism waxed slowly great through renunciation, inertia and mystical contemplation; but Jehovah and Allah were made of sterner stuff. It seems probable that, despite the peaceful creed and practice of its founder, Christianity would never have become a serious rival of other world-faiths had it not been for the implacable swords of Constantine and Charlemagne; but Islam was fortunate from the beginning in that its inventor entertained no silly scruples about blood-letting. The Crusades, the French Revolution, and Cromwellian Puritanism were attended by an amount of sadism that may well make one pause before too severely condemning the blood-mania and sex-obsession that mark every stage of Islam's triumphant progress.

Thus it happened that, from December, 622, until October, 623, the Prophet sent six separate expeditions against the Meccan caravans. The first three were entirely unsuccessful, notwithstanding the fact that Mohammed presented the leader of each one with a white banner mounted on a staff; but the fourth, led by the Prophet himself, was marked by a momentous incident. Though he failed to capture his prey, he made some sort of offensive and defensive alliance with the idolatrous tribe of Banu Damrah; and, apparently lest he might be rightly criticized for making friends with unbelievers, he justified his action in the only acceptable way—by a revelation. "It may be that Allah will bring about friendship between you and those whom you hold to be your enemies. . . . Allah does not forbid you respecting those who have not made war against you on account of (your) religion, and have not driven you forth from your homes. . . . Allah only forbids you respecting those who made war against you on account of (your) religion, and drove you forth from your homes. . . ." It may be surmised that the Prophet, himself an ex-camel-driver familiar with Bedouin ways, was moved to speak thus by two considerations: desert tribes that subsisted principally by plunder would be quick to appreciate the desirability of linking themselves with a faith that sanctified theft here and promised Paradise hereafter; besides, a successful assault on Koreish merchandise could hardly be made without the acquiescence or assistance of the tribes through whose territory that merchandise passed.

The fifth expedition was fruitless, but the sixth brought about alliances with several seashore clans; and a seventh one led not only to the first actual bloodshed, but to an even more striking innovation. Two days before the end of the sacred month of Rejeb, Mohammed sent eight men forth and gave their leader sealed orders which were not to be opened until after a two days' march. By a mere coincidence or by a sly design of the Prophet, the document was thus read, according to instructions, on the last day of Rejeb. After commanding the leader not to force "any of thy followers against his inclination," it ordered him to lie in wait for a Meccan caravan. Faced by the dilemma of fighting when strife was taboo, or of delaying until it would be too late to overtake the Koreish travelers, the Moslems summarily solved the problem by shooting an arrow through one of the Meccans and returning to Medina with the booty. Then, to their utter dismay, Mohammed rose up, "his face red with anger," and declared, "I never commanded thee to fight in the Sacred month." Yet it is curiously interesting to note that this heavenly message soon appeared: "They will ask thee concerning the Sacred months, whether they may war therein. Say: Warring therein is grievous; but to obstruct the way of God and to deny Him, to hinder men from the Holy temple, and to expel His people thence, that is more grievous with God."

Thus, through blind caprice or far-seeing, statesmanlike duplicity, the way was opened for bloodshed on a grand and wholly unrestricted scale. Nine centuries before Machiavelli, and eleven before Napoleon, the Prophet of Islam formulated this dictum: "War after all is but a game of deception." Deception of several kinds, that is to say: one's foes should be openly cursed and belittled while privately they were respected and even feared; one's followers should be assured that martial ardor was the best of all possible virtues and that death on the field of honor was a matchless boon. "The sword," Mohammed declared, "is the key of Heaven and Hell; a drop of blood shed in the cause of God, a night spent in arms, is of more avail than two months of fasting or prayer; whosoever falls in battle, his sins are forgiven; at the day of judgment his wounds shall be resplendent as vermilion, and odiferous as musk; and the loss of his limbs shall be supplied by the wings of angels and cherubim." The Koran of this period teems with frightful maledictions against the Koreish, and transcendent pictures of the Paradise that awaited the Moslem elect. Those warriors who could repeat the greatest number of its verses were, we are told, rewarded with the pick of the spoil after a victorious contest, and those who fell martyrs to Islam were buried with the most honorable rites. It was only too easy, one suspects, for devout Moslem warriors to memorize such passages as these: "War is ordained for you, even if it be irksome unto you. Perchance ye may dislike that which is good for you, and love that which is evil for you. But God knoweth, and ye know not. . . . God loveth not the Transgressors. Kill them whereso-ever ye find them; and expel them from whence they have expelled you. . . . Those of you that contribute before the victory, and fight, shall not be placed on the same level, but shall have a rank superior over those who contribute after it and fight. Who is he that lendeth unto the Lord a goodly loan? He shall double the same, and he shall have honorable recompense. . . . Those that have gone into exile for the cause of God, and then have been slain, or have died, We shall certainly nourish them with an excellent provision, for God is the best Provider. . . . He shall lead them into the Paradise whereof He hath told them. . . For ever therein—a fair abode and resting place!"

II

So it came to pass that the Prophet, who had managed to survive at Mecca only because of the Koreishite respect for ties of blood, was himself responsible for starting a blood-feud against the Koreish. He appears, however, to have been far less disturbed by this consideration than by the fact that he had not yet succeeded in winning any considerable amount of loot from them; but his desire was soon to be amply gratified.

In the autumn of 623, Abu Sufyan, a leading Meccan merchant, had conducted the most important caravan of the year to Syria, and in January, 624, he was on his way home with fifty thousand pieces of gold.

Mohammed had meanwhile determined that this rich cargo should be his; but, being yet somewhat inexperienced in the niceties of brigandage and slaughter, he carelessly allowed rumors of his intention to reach the ears of Abu, who at once sent a runner to Mecca with an urgent request for a rescuing force. The Prophet, in the meanwhile, rallied his supporters for the assault after this fashion: "See! here cometh a caravan of Koreish in which they have embarked much wealth. Come! let us go forth; peradventure the Lord will enrich us with the same." Scores of refugees and citizens gladly leaped forth to obey, but he would allow none save the righteous to join him. Chancing to spy two heathens among the volunteers, he sternly addressed them thus, "None shall go forth with me but he who is of our Faith." To their plea that they were redoubtable fighters who would ask nothing but their share of the plunder, he replied: "Ye shall not go thus. *Believe and fight!*" Immediately they asserted their profound conviction that he was indeed the Prophet of Allah, whereupon their ears were gladdened with the remark, "Now go forth and fight!" And these two became such famous despoilers that another heathen, after noting how greatly their conversion had benefited them, sadly exclaimed: "Would that I had gone forth with the Prophet! Then I had surely secured large booty!"

After dispatching two scouts to watch the movements of the caravan, Mohammed and his army of three hundred and five men at once set out toward Bedr (a spot near the coast to the southwest of Medina), hoping to apprehend the caravan at that place. While on the way, he deliberately avoided passing through certain localities whose names were unpleasing to him; for this singular man, who commonly appeared morose, taciturn and phlegmatic, had a nervous temperament that was extraordinarily susceptible to an astonishing variety of idiosyncratic fancies and whims. He would not sit down at night in a dark room; he believed that odd numbers had greater virtue than even ones; he changed color and walked nervously around during heavy storms; and he had a charmingly ingenuous faith in portents. Abu Sufyan, too, believed in signs—when they meant something definite. When he came to a well at Bedr, his eagle eyes spied two ominous datestones that the careless scouts had dropped near its brink. "Camels from Yathrib!" cried Abu; "these be the scouts of Mohammed!" and he immediately guided his caravan at full speed to the right.

His runner meanwhile had reached Mecca where, approaching the Kaba, he forced his camel to kneel; then, cutting off its nose and ears and tearing his shirt-tails to signify that a dreadful calamity impended, the Arabian Paul Revere screamed: "Koreish! Koreish! your caravan is pursued by Mohammed. Help! oh help!" The Meccans, already enraged at the murder of their tribesman at the hands of Moslems during Rejeb, were more than eager for vengeance, and an army of about nine hundred and fifty men at once started for Bedr. But, when they neared that place, a messenger reached them with the news that the caravan had fled on and was already out of danger. A heated discussion arose as to what should be done: since their merchandise was safe, should they return; or, should they take up the presumptuous challenge of the renegade Prophet? While both points of view were being violently argued, another scout came rushing up with the appalling information that the Moslem "numbers are small, but death is astride upon the camels of Yathrib." Following this alarming prophecy, a retreat had almost been ordered when Abu Jahl, the nasty girl-slapper, taunted his compatriots by calling them cowards, and bade one Amir, a brother of the murdered Meccan, to think of his brother-blood; Amir immediately tore off his garments, covered himself with dust and began to shriek his brother's name aloud. Thus their fury was revived, and, though a few craven-hearted ones returned to Mecca, the rest marched posthaste toward the oncoming foe.

During this time the news of the enemy's advance had reached the army of Mohammed; but, instead of causing debate, it had roused the Moslem enthusiasm to a greater pitch. The citizens, too, even though they had not pledged themselves to assist in offensive warfare, were equally affected. "Prophet of the Lord!" shouted their leader, "march whither thou listest; encamp wheresoever thou mayest choose; make war or conclude peace with whom thou wilt. For I swear by Him who hath sent thee the Truth, that if thou wert to march till our camels fell down dead, we should go forward with thee to the world's end." Then Mohammed, deeply affected by this proof of devotion, responded: "Go forward with the blessing of God! For, verily, He hath promised one of the two—the army or the caravan—that He will deliver it into our hands. By the Lord! methinks I even now see the battlefield strewn with dead." Here were no timid bickerings, no half-hearted counsels, no unmanly scruples about spilling fraternal blood: what *was* there to fear when Paradise, revenge for ostracism, and fifty thousand shining pieces of gold beckoned them on? And the Prophet, who never did things by halves, fanned the rising fires of fanaticism by giving turbulent utterance to a series of commingled imprecatory and suppliant prayers. "O Lord! let not

Abu Jahl escape, the Pharaoh of his people! Lord! let not Zaama escape; rather let the eyes of his father run sore for him with weeping, and become blind! . . . O Lord! I beseech thee, forget not Thy promise of assistance and of victory. O Lord! if this little band be vanquished, Idolatry will prevail, and the pure worship of Thee cease from off the earth!"

When night fell, both armies had nearly reached Bedr. Mohammed and Abu Bekr sought repose in a hut of palm branches guarded by a soldier with his sword drawn; and the Prophet's slumbers were comforted by dreams in which the enemy appeared as a pitifully weak force. Morning had barely dawned when foe swiftly advanced to meet foe. A providential rain had softened the ground over which the Koreish must needs pass, and, at the same time, it had paradoxically hardened the soil beneath the Moslem feet; the fortunate fact that small sandy ridges concealed the majority of the Meccans induced the Medinese to advance with extra courage; and the Koreish suffered the further disadvantage of facing the troublesome rays of the rising sun. In addition, the Prophet's superior foresight, abetted by the suggestion of a counselor, had prompted him to take possession of a never-failing spring, as well as to destroy all the other available water-sources; for he always backed up his incessant prayers by using every device of military tactics that he happened to know, or acquire.

According to the Arabian custom, the fray opened with a series of individual combats. Three Meccan warriors stepped vaingloriously forth, daring the three best men among the Moslems to face them; and valorous Hamza, impetuous Ali, and Obeida the septuagenarian rushed forward to accept the challenge. The swords of Hamza and Ali soon dripped with the life-blood of two Koreishites; when Obeida fell severely wounded, they sprang to his aid and simultaneously delivered two lusty strokes that killed the third. Then, raising the cry, "Ye conquerors, strike!" the serried Moslem ranks hurled themselves against the enemy; but the Prophet himself, while the deadly yet indecisive struggle was being waged, played an ambiguous part. Friendly traditions state that he bounded about with a sword in his hand. Those of another sort relate that, upon observing the first shedding of blood, he retired to his hut and swooned; that, upon being revived, he poured forth the most energetic prayers; and that, even before the battle commenced, he had taken pains to have a swift camel tied to his tent as a last resource against the possible calamity of defeat. Still other narratives assert that he occupied himself principally in reminding his accomplices that Paradise awaited those who perished for Islam—a promise whose validity he himself seems to have been indisposed to test. For Mohammed, no less than many other religiously-minded emperors and tsars, appears to have conducted himself in battle according to the wise principle that a head without a halo is infinitely more desirable than a halo without a head.

While the disorderly Meccan forces were being steadily pressed back by the close-joined Moslem ranks, a furious storm of wind arose. Until this time, Mohammed seems to have been rather sceptical concerning the issue of his prayers; but, now that the foe was beginning to waver, he doubted no longer. "That," he exclaimed while the tempest raged, "is Gabriel with a thousand angels charging down upon the foe." Then, stooping and grabbing up a handful of small stones, he rose and hurled them at the Koreish, accompanying his action with the shout, "Confusion seize their faces!" This double assault, timed at the psychological moment, could not fail to have effect. The broken and shaken Meccan ranks—thoroughly discomfited by a lack of discipline, by a merely lukewarm interest in fighting their quondam neighbors and friends, and, as their own satirists abundantly pointed out later, by actual cowardice—cracked apart and fled in complete dismay, to be harassed and killed or captured by the pursuing Moslems. Mohammed lost but fourteen men in the encounter, whereas more than a hundred Koreish were slain or taken prisoners.

Curious scenes followed. A Moslem named Moadh had succeeded in cutting off Abu Jahl's leg. Just then Moadh, attacked by Abu's son, had found himself with one of his own arms almost severed; and, realizing that this member was now a useless impediment, Moadh bent over, placed his foot on the injured arm, wrenched it off, and continued to fight. At this moment one Abdallah came running up to assist Moadh, and, overjoyed at his good fortune in stumbling over such a notorious enemy, cut off Abu Jahl's head and carried it to Mohammed. The Prophet, who was just beginning to celebrate his victory, raised the exultant shout: "The head of the enemy of God! God! there is none other God!" "There is none other!" agreed Abdallah, dropping his gory prize before Mohammed's feet; and Abdallah almost fainted from bliss when the Prophet continued, "It is more acceptable to me than the choicest camel in all Arabia." It happened, also, that Ali had overheard Mohammed praying for the death of Naufal ibn Khuweilid, who had been taken prisoner; so Ali ran up, coolly slaughtered him, and promptly hastened with the good news to the Prophet, who joyously commented that this was doubtless a direct answer to his supplication. The spoil was soon gathered, and a pit was dug into which the Koreishite bodies were tossed; and Mohammed, who stood by watching the proceedings, greeted each corpse by name, adding this question, "Have ye now found true that which your Lord did promise you? What my Lord promised me, that verily I have found to be true." "O Prophet!" inquired an amazed observer, "dost thou speak unto the dead?" "Yea, verily," was the reply, "for now they well know that the promise of their Lord hath fully come to pass."

Next morning, when the prisoners were led before him, he turned a malignant gaze upon Al-Nadr, who had been captured by Mikdad. "There is death in that glance," the frightened Al-Nadr whispered to a bystander, and he was right; his trembling plea for mercy was rewarded with the response, "Islam hath rent all bonds asunder," from a prominent Moslem, and with the command, "Strike off his head!" from Mohammed, who also felt moved to add, "And, O Lord, do Thou of Thy bounty grant unto Mikdad a better prey than this!" Another prisoner, Okba—a man well versed in Grecian, Persian and Arabian lore, who is said to have aroused the Prophet's ire by the observation that, if a fund of good stories entitled a man to call himself a prophet, he was fully as good a candidate as Mohammed himself—was likewise ordered to face his doom. Mohammed, however, first satisfied Okba's curiosity as to why he had been singled out for destruction with the words, "Because of thine enmity to God and his Prophet." "And my little girl," continued Okba, "who will take care of her?" "Hell-fire!" was the swift reply, as Okba was chopped to the ground. The Prophet, surveying the remains, rejoiced after this fashion: "I give thanks unto the Lord that hath slain thee, and comforted mine eyes thereby." Yet it should be stated that the defenders of Islam asseverate that Mohammed's remarks to the Koreishite corpses were intended to express pity rather than hatred, and that the ejaculation "Hell-fire!" was a reference to the fact that Okba's children were nicknamed "children of fire"—in other words, he implied that Okba's descendants would be cared for by his relatives.

Whatever the facts may be, it is certain that Mohammed treated the rest of the captives with a kindness rarely matched in the martial history of Arabia. While the implacable Omar made a violent plea for their summary death, and while the easy-going Abu Bekr urged clemency, Gabriel winged his way from Allah's presence with the gratifying information that Mohammed might do as he wished; but he added the portentous remark that, if the Koreish were spared, a like number of Moslems would perish in battle within the year. Mohammed eventually pleased everyone, except Omar, by announcing that the prisoners would not be slain, but that they could be freed only by ransom, and that those Moslems who might fall as Gabriel had foretold would "inherit Paradise and the crown of martydom." His decision was probably reached on account of several considerations: the ransom for some seventy prisoners might benefit Islam even more than their blood; there was the further chance that some of them might become disciples; and, finally, he may conceivably have been more mercifully minded than his traducers admit.

Joy and thanksgiving were unbounded when the news of the overwhelming victory reached Medina; even the toddling children chased around the streets crying out, "Abu Jahl, the sinner, is slain!" The prisoners were so kindly treated that some of them actually became converts, while the stubborn remainder were ransomed for reasonable sums—except those whose wealth Mohammed's abnormally retentive memory still kept in mind. Thus, when the case of the opulent Naufal, Mohammed's own cousin, came up, the Prophet amazed him with a demand for the thousand spears that he possessed; Naufal was so completely upset by this evidence of what appeared to be supernatural assistance that he is said to have accepted Islam on the spot. Among the prisoners, also, was the Prophet's rich uncle Al-Abbas, who declined to pay on the ground that he was already a Moslem and that he had been obliged to fight against his conscience. "God knows best about that," replied his nephew; "externally you were against us, so ransom yourself." When Al-Abbas demurred, saying that he was now penniless, he was met with the pitiless query, "Then where is the money which, when you left Mecca, you secretly deposited with your wife?" Al-Abbas paid his ransom. Meanwhile a spirited discussion arose as to the way in which the booty—which included about one hundred and fifty camels and horses, together with vast quantities of vestments and armor—should be divided; the matter, indeed, was so important that it could be settled only by a heavenly decree, which stipulated that one-fifth should be placed at the disposal of "God and the Prophet" and the remainder equally dispersed among the army.

But these were mere mercenary considerations. The outstanding, overshadowing fact was that a small body of Moslems had utterly routed a force three times their own number. Mohammed might well claim that he had at last performed a veritable miracle, and his subordinates might well have become a little vainglorious too; but the Koran soon placed the credit for the "Day of Deliverance" where it properly belonged. "As for victory, it is from none other than from God; for God is glorious and wise. . . . And ye slew them not, but God slew them. Neither was it thou, O Prophet, that didst cast the gravel; but God did cast it." And yet the human side of the encounter was not neglected. The glorious Three Hundred who had fought and conquered such superior odds thenceforth became the peerage of Medina. Until the end of his life, Mohammed was willing to forgive almost any sort of offence committed by any one of them, for, as he wisely declared, he could not be sure that Allah Himself had not given them free leave to do as they chose.

At Mecca, however, very different scenes were witnessed. The bitter pangs of shame and despair that everyone felt upon learning of the stunning defeat soon gave way to a fiery thirst for vengeance. For a month this frenzy reigned; then human nature intervened and a universal lament for the dead ascended, for almost every home in Mecca had been bereaved. A harrowing yet beautiful story illustrates how the grim self-restraint of the Koreish was finally broken. One night an aged father, who had lost two sons, heard the sound of weeping and thus commanded his servant: "Go see! It may be that Koreish have begun to wail for their dead; perchance I too may wail, for grief consumeth me within." Informed that it was only a woman who was mourning for her strayed camel, he poured forth an impassioned threnody. "Doth she weep for her camel, and for it banish sleep from her eyes? Nay, if we will weep, let us weep over Bedr—weep for Okeil, and for Al-Harith the lion of lions!" Perhaps the Koreish now realized the irreparable and fatal error they had made in deciding to take Mohammed seriously. Had they persisted in their original intention—mocked at him as an idle dreamer and a crack-brained idiot—he might have lived and died harmlessly in Mecca. But persecution had proved to be his best friend: forced to defend himself and to become the head of a little protecting army, he had revealed an unsuspected military acumen that had reduced his hostile kinsmen to this desperate condition. One Spartan couple in Mecca, however, refused to join in the common woe. "Weep not for your slain, mourn not their loss, neither let the bard bewail their fate," was the stern advice of Abu Sufyan. "If ye lament with elegies, it will ease your wrath and diminish your enmity toward Mohammed and his fellows. And, should that reach their ears, and they laugh at us, will not their scorn be worse than all? Haply the turn may come, and ye may yet obtain your revenge. As for me, I will touch no oil, neither approach my wife, until I shall have gone forth again to fight with Mohammed." And when Abu's wife, Hind, was chided for refusing to wail for her father, brother and uncle, she fiercely responded: "Nay, I will not weep until ye again wage war with Mohammed and his fellows. If tears could wipe the grief from off my heart, I too would weep as ye; but it is not thus with Hind." Not to be outdone by her husband, she too declared that she would neither use oil nor approach her marital couch until an avenging Meccan army was on the march.

III

Elated at his astounding success, the Prophet occupied the following year in consolidating his gains and extending his influence. Meanwhile he continued to pay an exorbitant amount of homage to Allah, the Giver of all good; but, in starting a universal espionage system in Medina and in assuming an ever more menacing attitude toward unbelievers and Jews, he appears to have acted solely on his own responsibility. Nor were the Koreish idle during this year. As time slowly mitigated their poignant suffering, their business instincts revived and new trade routes were mapped out; the profits that accrued therefrom were stored up against the eagerly awaited day when a fearful retribution should be inflicted upon their murderous kinsmen. Abu Sufyan, who was chafing under the irksome restrictions of his vow, actually succeeded in destroying some enemy property and in slaying two Moslems; but when he joyfully hastened back to Mecca, under the impression that he had earned the dissolution of his oath, he discovered much to his chagrin that Hind did not agree with him. The Moslems, irritated because the Koreish had gained even such a slight success, retaliated by capturing a caravan that yielded one hundred thousand pieces of silver; yet, when the news of this added indignity reached the Meccans, it only steeled their already inflexible determination—the moment for a swift and terrible vengeance had come.

Plans for a crushing campaign against the Moslems were drawn up; and all the Koreishites strained every nerve to expedite the martial plans and keep them secret—all of them, that is, except Al-Abbas, who, for some inexplicable reason, still retained a sneaking affection for the hard-hearted nephew who had forced him to pay such a stiff ransom. So it happened that, while Mohammed was communing with Allah in the Mosque during January, 625, a sealed letter, conveying the dreadful news that three thousand Koreish, including seven hundred warriors in armor and two hundred cavalry, were ready to march upon Medina, was handed to him. Despite the strongest efforts of the Prophet to keep this information secret, it leaked out and caused tremendous excitement and confusion. On this occasion, Mohammed's perpetually-recurring dreams portended a defeat—he imagined that his sword was broken. A public meeting was called to discuss the ominous situation; and, according to some authorities, the Prophet related his dream, which he interpreted thus: "The fracture in my sword portendeth an injury to myself," adding that it would be wisest to remain within the fortified walls of Medina. The elder Moslems agreed with their leader, but the young Hotspurs arose in violent opposition: they asserted that they would not "sit quietly here, a laughing-stock to all Arabia," but would "go forth and smite our foes, even as we did at Bedr." The headstrong impetuosity of youth prevailed, and Mohammed at length acceded. After preaching a strong discourse, in which he assured them, "If ye be steadfast, the Lord will grant you victory," he retired to his house, whence he shortly emerged dressed in helmet and mail, with a sword hanging from his girdle. This sight deeply distressed the Moslems, for it appeared that their commander was at last going to risk his life on the battlefield; they therefore begged that he would follow his first counsel and remain within Medina's walls. But he sternly replied: "I invited you to this and ye would not. It becometh not a prophet, when once he hath girded himself to the battle, to lay his armor down again until the Lord hath decided betwixt him and his enemies. Wait, therefore, on the Lord. Only be steadfast, and He will send you victory."

The talismanic effect of these words was immediate, and the Moslem army at once took to the field. It is not clear whether Abdallah ibn Obei, at the head of three hundred unbelievers, actually joined this army and then deserted when it was on the march; for some think that he never joined it at all. Mohammed is represented as having forbidden the unbelievers to assist him, saying that he did not desire "the aid of Unbelievers to fight against the unbelieving"; though other accounts maintain that Abdallah and his followers sallied forth with the faithful, but deserted at first sight of the enemy. Again, it is possible that Abdallah never manifested any desire to fight at all—that the tales both of his reprimand and desertion were invented by the Moslems in order to emphasize the smallness of their force. It was small enough, at all events, for barely seven hundred Moslems went forth to face a foe more than four times their own number. The Koreish had meanwhile circled the city, until they drew up for battle near the hill of Uhud, three miles to the north; and there the army of Allah met them.

There can be little doubt that, had the plan devised

by Mohammed been followed, a victory, or at least a draw, would have been his. Realizing that success against such overwhelming odds could be gained only by far superior tactics and stratagems, he issued three imperative commands. He instructed fifty sharpshooters to remain, at all costs, on a little hill nearby, and prevent any effort of the Koreishite cavalry to attack from the rear—"stir not from this spot; if ye see us pursuing and plundering the enemy, join not with us; if we be pursued and even worsted, do not venture to our aid"—he enjoined upon his prayer-trained troops the imperious necessity of keeping their serried lines intact; and he forbade them to advance until he gave the order, for he rightly believed that, so long as his force cohered, it would be impregnable. But the Prophet was destined to learn that, once a body of men has tasted the sweets of pillage and rapine, it is very likely not only to forget its religious professions but to disobey its own commander. When these admirable arrangements had been made, he cautiously donned a second coat of armor and sedately awaited for the foe to make the first move.

It was not long in coming. All at once the whole Koreishite force began to advance, while a group of women, headed by the bloodthirsty Hind and beating timbrels and drums, preceded the men and accompanied their rude music with stirring songs that promised special favors for the brave and threatened unbearable calamities for the timid.

> "Daughters of the brave are we,
> On carpets step we delicately;
> Boldly advance, and we embrace you!
> Turn your backs and we will shun you—
> Shun you with disdain."

Then the Meccan champions, ardently desiring to win favor in the eyes of their martial females, rushed forth and dared individual Moslems to engage them in the customary single combat—an invitation that was right gladly accepted. And now the history of Bedr was temporarily repeated, for a succession of Koreishites fell before the superior efficiency of Allah's favorites. At first dismayed, and then angered, by the swift fate of their leading standard-bearers, the Meccan force hurled itself at the Moslem array; but its inflexible front withstood the desperate assault, while the unerring archers, stationed on the little hill, prevented the Koreishite cavalry from disrupting the Moslem left wing. The Meccans wavered, cracked apart, turned irresolutely, and fled in ignominious haste, while the jubilant Medinese, headed by their two heroes, Ali and Hamza, bounded hotly after the pusillanimous fugitives.

But, just at this moment, the validity of Gabriel's

warning after Bedr became manifest. Certain of their success, the Moslem ranks broke up and began to despoil the enemy camp; and this gratifying spectacle, which was seen by the archers, was too compelling to be resisted. Uttering anticipatory shouts of glee, they deserted their post and came running to join in the general fun. And then the situation speedily changed. No longer held at bay by a withering discharge of arrows, the Meccan cavalry whirled suddenly around and came smashing through the Moslem rear. Among others the great Hamza fell, mortally wounded by a javelin from the hand of a hired assassin. Hind, whose father had been slain by Hamza at Bedr, had bribed her Ethiopian slave, Wahshi, with the promise of freedom should he lay Hamza low; and his body had hardly ceased to quiver before Hind pounced savagely upon it, ripped out his liver, which she tore to pieces with her teeth, and collected his nails and fragments of skin to make bracelets for her arms and legs. The Medinese, taken completely by surprise and terror-stricken at the death of their greatest warrior, incontinently abandoned their arms and stolen property and began to run even faster than the Koreish had done a few moments earlier.

When Mohammed observed this calamitous reversal, he tried to rally his fleeing forces by expostulation. "Whither away?" he shouted; "Come back! I am the

Apostle of God! Return!" But the Moslems were much more interested just then in saving their skins than in any number of prophets or gods; so Mohammed, for the first time in his career, was forced to fight for his life. We learn that he discharged arrows until his bow broke, whereupon he madly hurled stones about, and may possibly have killed one Meccan; yet, even in his dire extremity, he did not forget to make vehement promises of an incomparable reward in Paradise to any Moslem who would keep the foe off his own person. But his under lip was wounded, one of his front teeth was broken, and a furious stroke drove his helmet-rings into his cheek. Then, either because he was really stunned or exceptionally clever, he fell to the ground apparently dead, while among the Koreish the glad cry "Mohammed is slain!" resounded far and wide. Complete confusion seized the Moslems when they heard this appalling shout, and in their consternation they shrieked aloud, "Where now is the promise of his Lord?" Yet this very circumstance probably saved them from an utter rout, for the Koreish, certain of the Prophet's decease, believed that their main object was attained and accordingly failed to take advantage of the victory that lay so easily within their grasp.

For Mohammed, in fact, was still very much alive. When this unbelievably good news spread, his confederates could not refrain from shouting it aloud; but, aware that he was yet in great danger, the Prophet peremptorily checked them. He was borne to a cave near by, where an attempt was made to care for his wounds; the helmet-rings had penetrated so deeply into his face that one poor fellow broke two teeth in a praiseworthy attempt to pull them out. Mohammed's courage had now come back to such an extent that he essayed to apostrophize his enemies thus: "How shall a people prosper that treat thus their Prophet who calleth them unto the Lord! Let the wrath of God burn against the men that have besprinkled the face of His Apostle with his own blood! Let not the year pass over them alive!" At the same time, however, he deemed it advisable to change armor with another Moslem, in case the Koreish might come to search for him; then, rejoining his followers outside the cave, he glared at the Meccans retreating in the distance.

Just at this moment Abu Sufyan, who, puffed with pride, had remained to taunt his discomfited foes, called out, "Mohammed! Abu Bekr! Omar!" and, hearing no response, shouted, "Then all are slain, and ye are rid of them!" This was too much for Omar to endure with equanimity; and so, disobeying the Prophet, he bellowed: "Thou liest! They are all alive, thou enemy of God, and will requite thee yet." Hearing this, Abu

Sufyan twitted Omar with these words: "Then this day shall be a return for Bedr. Fortune alternates as the bucket. Hearken! ye will find mutilated ones upon the field; this was not my desire, but neither am I displeased thereat. Glory to Al-Ozza! Glory to Hubal! Al-Ozza is ours, not yours!" It was now Mohammed's turn to be vexed, though he wisely entrusted his retort to Omar who, properly primed by his chief, exclaimed: "The Lord is ours; He is not yours!" Abu Sufyan, who thought that the argument was becoming rather childish, merely answered, "We shall meet after a year at Bedr." "Be it so!" growled Omar; and then Abu, together with Hind his spouse, made haste to return home so that they might mutually dissolve their twelve-months' oath.

Only twenty Koreish had been slain, whereas the stark bodies of seventy-four Moslems were stiffening on the battlefield. Thither Mohammed now betook himself, and, upon seeing Hamza's defiled corpse, he tugged angrily at his beard and swore that he would treat thirty Koreishite bodies in a similar way; but later he repented of this remark, and indeed issued stern orders forbidding his troops ever to mutilate a fallen enemy. The crumpled Moslem army then set out for Medina, for it was feared that the Koreish might decide to attack the defenseless city; but a scout soon came hastening up, shouting aloud the cheering news that the Koreish were hurrying southward toward Mecca. "Gently," Mohammed mildly chided him, "let us not appear before the people to rejoice at the departure of the enemy!" For the Prophet was already profoundly absorbed in meditating schemes that would enable him satisfactorily to explain his defeat. But just now the sense of loss excluded every other emotion from the minds of the refugees and allies—the explanations could wait. Mingled with the ubiquitous sorrow was a feeling of helpless insecurity: the Koreish might yet change their minds and retrace their steps; so a watch was stationed at the Prophet's door, behind which he went to sleep so soundly that he failed to obey Bilal's indefatigable call to evening prayers. The Meccans, however, who at this time had another easy opportunity to alter the map of the world, had decided that they had evened matters up with their kinsmen—and besides, they were much more interested in starting their remunerative caravans on the march again than in making or unmaking history.

Faced for the first time by an apparently irretrievable disaster, Mohammed well realized that not merely were his assumptions of sacerdotal preëminence, Allah Himself, and indeed all Islam, in imminent danger, but that his very existence would be at stake unless he proved able to satisfy the querulous clamors of his people and explain just how it was that he had failed. Never did his greatness reveal itself more splendidly than in this emergency; his every action was planned with the utmost care. His public demonstration of grief for Hamza, and his decision to visit the field of Uhud once a year to bless its Moslem martyrs—where, on each occasion, he regularly repeated the safe formula, "Peace be on you for that which ye endured, and a blessed futurity above!"—may have been genuine enough; at all events, such actions would be calculated to impress his underlings with his sincerity. But mutinous murmurs were now rampant: if Allah's arm had brought victory at Bedr, what was He doing on the day of Uhud? and in any case what was to be thought of the Prophet's multitudinous promises? Yet these apparently unanswerable complaints were no match for Mohammed's wily brain. The masterful orator kept silence until the time came when, as was customary on Friday, he made known the latest dispatches from Allah in the Mosque.

And there he held the complainers in the hollow of his hand. The time and the place itself, with its rude but impressive grandeur, its venerable associations, its atmosphere of religious awe, had been chosen with surpassing care; and, before a word had been uttered, the audience was unconsciously in a passive, hypnotic state. Then the Prophet, loosing every ounce of his tremendous nervous energy, poured forth a harangue in which subtle explanations, reproof, denunciation, self-justification, and finally mild praise and encouragement were blended with superb artistry. If Allah had conferred victory at Bedr, through the instrumentality of "the havoc-making angels," He had permitted a defeat at Uhud in order to separate the true believers from the hypocrites; then, too, Allah *had* been with them until they disobeyed the Prophet—"When you ran off precipitately, and did not wait for any one, and the Apostle was calling you from your rear." The cowardice of those who had stayed at home, as well as lust for loot, had also played a large part in the defeat; but the Prophet himself was blameless, for he had accepted the decision of a majority of Moslems as to where and how the battle should be fought. Nor had the Koreish gained by winning: "We grant them respite only that they may add to their sins; and they shall have a disgraceful chastisement." Furthermore, was it possible that the Moslems had forgotten that the dead were infinitely better off in Paradise?—where "No terror afflicteth them, neither are they grieved." And even if Mohammed, being only mortal like other men and "other Apostles that have gone before him," had been killed, Islam must still continue: "What! if he were to die or be killed, must ye needs turn back upon your heels?" And finally: "Be not cast down, neither be ye grieved. Ye shall yet be victorious if ye are true Believers."

When it was over, every shamefaced person present was thoroughly convinced that the Prophet, alone among the Moslems, was wholly guiltless, that Allah was more adorable than ever, and that the defeat at Uhud was an excellent example of a remarkably successful strategic retreat.

VII

DEFEAT OF ALL INFIDELS

I

Another year sped by, until the appointed time came for the Koreish and the Moslems to clash again at Bedr. A prolonged drought, however, had impaired the Meccan finances to such an extent that Abu Sufyan decided it would be advisable to postpone the engagement; so, summoning strategy to his aid, he caused a rumor to be diffused through Medina to the effect that the Koreish had equipped a vast army for the impending conflict. The Moslems, whose spirits had not yet recovered from the shock of Uhud, were so perturbed at this report that they were unwilling to venture forth; but Mohammed, whose espionage system had now penetrated even as far as the confines of Mecca and who, therefore, was probably aware of Abu Sufyan's ruse, swore a great oath that he would march to Bedr even though he marched alone. Shamed by their leader's heroism, the Medinese recovered their courage; and the Prophet, at the head of fifteen hundred men, set out for Bedr in the spring of 626. The Koreish also finally scraped up enough tepid enthusiasm to venture forth with an army of over two thousand men; but they soon turned back, so they later declared, because of the lack of provisions. Though the Moslems were by no means sorry to hear of this, they publicly boasted their contempt for the "water-gruel" force from Mecca; then, since it was the time of the annual fairs, they remained eight days at Bedr profiting greatly from the sale of the abundant wares they had carried in their train.

If, as it now appeared to Mohammed, the Koreish were disposed to keep the peace, the extended lull in hostilities would furnish an admirable opportunity to flaunt the banners of Islam over an ever widening extent of Arabia; for the defeat of Uhud, no less than the success at Bedr, had profoundly convinced him that the ultimate victory of Islam depended upon the sword. The Koran of this period breathes defiance against the enemies of Islam on almost every page; its profuse maledictions, once confined to the evildoers of Mecca, now include all unbelievers everywhere. All other things, even the hitherto unescapable performance of daily prayers, take second place to the relentless promulgation of the faith by military means. "When ye march abroad in the earth, it shall be no crime unto you that ye shorten your prayers, if ye fear that the Unbelievers may attack you." Such an inducement was remarkably well calculated to win over to the army those numerous believers who had discovered that five highly complicated daily contortions were a little irksome, and the Moslem force therefore grew by leaps and bounds. As a result, during the summer of 626 Mohammed was able to conduct a successful campaign as far north as the border of Syria—an event of incalculable import. For the first time the tentacles of Islam had stretched beyond the bounds of Arabia: the curtain had risen on the first scene of a world-wide drama that still awaits its last act.

It seems probable that these sweeping expeditions at length aroused the Arabians to the danger that threatened them all. At all events, in the early months of 627 it happened that a confederacy of Koreishite, Bedouin and Jewish tribes put an army numbering approximately ten thousand men in the field against Medina. The Prophet well knew that the memories of Uhud, still rankling in the minds of his compatriots, made it highly inexpedient to desert the city and meet the oncoming foe in the open field. Yet Medina must be defended at all costs—everyone, even the most feeble-kneed, was agreed upon that—and feverish counsels were held to devise a plan whereby the city might be made impregnable against assault. At this crucial juncture, a Persian ex-slave suggested that the city be entrenched in the same way as, in his travels, he had observed that the Mesopotamian cities were protected. Acting immediately upon his inspired advice, the Moslems filled in the gaps between their outer line of stone houses with a stone wall; and, at the southeastern quarter, which was entirely defenseless, a deep and wide ditch was dug. After six days of prodigious and incessant labor, the trench was completed. The Prophet threw himself heartily into the work, and, dirty and weary as he was, joined his stentorian voice in unison with the other toilers as they once again intoned the words:

> "O Lord! there is no happiness but that of Futurity.
> O Lord! have mercy on the Citizens and the Refugees!"

The result was that, when Abu Sufyan came marching up at the head of his conglomerate force, all that he could do was to permit his troops to shoot some harmless showers of arrows, pitch his tents, sit down, and wait for the Moslems to come forth. Entrenchments as a military device were entirely unknown in Arabia; so the invaders logically concluded that Mohammed was not a good sport—as on other occasions, he had violated the Arabic code of chivalry by proving that he had brains. "Truly this ditch is the artifice of strangers," they yelled, "a shift to which no Arab yet has ever stooped!" But the Moslems did not take the hint, and so next day the besiegers made a gallantly unsuccessful attempt to rush the barricade by sheer weight of numbers. Nevertheless, the assault accomplished one very irritating thing: for a whole day the devoutest of the Moslems had been prevented from saying their prayers. Gratifying amends for this forced neglect of Allah, however, were made when night fell; at that time an individual service was held for each omitted supplication, and Mohammed contributed a special comminatory request: "They have kept us from our daily prayers; God fill their bellies and their graves with fire!" Indeed, while the siege lasted, the Prophet spent most of the hours in protracted prayer, though he managed to find time enough to guard himself against the threatening activities of the Jews and other disaffected Medinese. Nor did his devices stop here. He even tried to buy off the Bedouins by promising them a third of the fruit from Medina's date-trees; but his leading allies, the Aus and the Khazraj, opposed his trickiness and admonished him to "give nothing unto them but the sword." Mohammed then played his trump card: if war was but a game of deception, why should he not skillfully divide the enemy against themselves? He instructed a trusty go-between to spread dissension among the foe by persuading the Bedouins and Jews in turn that their interests were mutually opposed. The scheme worked without a hitch, for the attacking forces, already discouraged by the cold, the difficulty of obtaining food, and the protracted delay, were ready to leave on any excuse. As a result, when a chilling storm of wind and rain incommoded them on the fifteenth day, they folded their tents and silently stole away. "Break up the camp and march," commanded Abu Sufyan. "As for myself I am gone"—and he suited his action to his words by clambering hastily upon his camel and trying to urge it away while its fore leg was still hitched.

Scarcely had the last camel disappeared when the Prophet, after thanking Allah for his timely assistance in sending the storm, was visited by Gabriel. "What!" chided the tireless angel, "hast thou laid aside thine armor, while as yet the angels have not laid theirs aside! Arise! go up against the Beni Koreiza." This Jewish tribe, which inhabited a fortress several miles southeast of Medina, had been the last to succumb to the blandishments of Abu Sufyan, but had finally yielded and taken part in the assault on Medina; so Mohammed made haste to obey the celestial behest, even though he had previously borrowed from the Beni Koreiza the picks and shovels with which the trench had been excavated. Heading three thousand soldiers, he immediately marched to the Jewish stronghold where, inasmuch as it was marvelously protected by nature rather than its inhabitants, he found it necessary to keep guard for several weeks. In the end the Jews agreed to surrender on condition that the Aus, their supposed allies, should decide their fate. To this Mohammed agreed, and the Aus, almost with one voice, demanded that the Beni Koreiza should be treated gently; yet they signified their willingness to abide by the decision of their chief, a huge, corpulent fellow named Sa'd.

Now it chanced that Sa'd, suffering from an arrow-wound inflicted during the late siege, was not in a pleasant frame of mind; and it has been surmised that Mohammed may have craftily reckoned on this very fact. "Proceed with thy judgment!" he commanded Sa'd. "Will ye, then," inquired Sa'd of his tribesmen, "bind yourselves by the covenant of God that whatsoever I shall decide, ye will accept?" After they had murmured their assent, he spoke. "My judgment is that the men shall be put to death, the women and children sold into slavery, and the spoil divided amongst the army." A torrent of objections was about to be poured forth, when the Prophet savagely commanded silence. "Truly the judgment of Sa'd is the judgment of God," he declared, "pronounced on high from beyond the Seventh Heaven." Trenches were dug that night, and next morning some seven or eight hundred men were marched out, forced to seat themselves in rows along the top of the trenches, were forthwith beheaded, and then tumbled into the long, gaping grave; the Prophet meanwhile looked on until, tiring of the monotonous spectacle, he departed to amuse himself with a Jewess whose husband had just perished. But poor Sa'd did not live long to enjoy his revenge; barely had he reached home when his wounds re-opened and he soon breathed his last. As he lay dying, the Prophet held him in his arms and prayed thus: "O Lord! Verily Sa'd hath labored in thy service. He hath believed in thy Prophet, and hath fulfilled his covenant. Wherefore do thou, O Lord, receive his spirit with the best reception wherewith thou receivest a departing soul!" Mohammed also helped to carry the coffin which, the bearers noted, was remarkably light for so heavy a man; but the Prophet explained the matter to the satisfaction of all. "The angels are carrying the bier, therefore it is light in your hands. Verily the throne on high doth vibrate for Sa'd, and the portals of heaven are opened, and he is attended by seventy thousand angels that never trod the earth before."

II

Busily occupied though he had been for several years with the gradual subjugation of the Koreish, Mohammed had yet found time to compel a motley group of less important enemies to bow meekly beneath the yoke of Islam. The extinction of the Beni Koreiza had been but one link in the long chain of his conquests. His Meccan kinsmen had naturally been the first to be imperiously brushed aside; but other temporary impediments had occasionally blocked his way.

Among them the few Christians who were scattered here and there throughout Arabia were of least moment. Split asunder as they were into various warring sects—the Monothelites, Jacobites, Melchites and Nestorians—they worried the Prophet but little; he seems to have regarded them with a tolerant and mildly amused eye. Having had scanty intercourse with them, he was probably quite ignorant of their disputatious creeds; therefore, while the Koran always speaks respectfully of the Saviour, Who is invariably designated "Jesus, Son of Mary," it makes many deplorable errors when it discusses the tenets and theogony of Christianity. It expressly denies that Jesus is the Son of God and completely repudiates the established doctrine of the Holy Trinity: "Wherefore believe in God, and in the Apostles; and say not, *There are Three.* Refrain: it will be better for you. Verily the Lord is one God. Glory be to Him! far be it from Him, that there should be to Him a Son." And Mohammed seems to have made the even more egregious error of supposing that the Trinity which he condemned was composed of the Father, Jesus and Mary; for the Koran utterly fails to recognize the incontrovertible existence of the Holy Ghost. Thus, while it has been reasonably urged that the Prophet both comprehended and hated Roman Catholicism, it may just as plausibly be argued that the conception of the Holy Spirit as a separate and distinct entity was too subtle for his eminently practical mind to grasp.

With Judaism, however, the case was very different. Though the Koran might place Christ on par with Abraham, Moses, David and other Hebrew prophets, it was to the customs and rites of the Jews that Mohammed paid obeisance rather than to those that had clustered around Christianity. Scarcely had he taken up his residence in Medina when he deliberately humbled himself in an effort to placate and win over the Jews; for, knowing their numbers and their power, he strongly desired to enter into a lasting union with them. To that end, he bound himself and his adherents to the Jews in a contract whose obligations were relatively mutual: "The Jews will profess their religion, the Moslems theirs. . . No one shall go forth to war excepting with the permission of Mohammed; but this shall not hinder any from seeking lawful revenge. . . If attacked, each shall come to the assistance of the other. . . War and Peace shall be made in common." There is also every reason to suppose that the command promulgated by Allah, when the Prophet visited Him in the Seventh Heaven, to the effect that all loyal Moslems must henceforth direct their prayers five times daily toward Jerusalem, was given because Mohammed expected that the Jews, seeing the Moslems thus busily engaged, would be insidiously flattered and insensibly led to look favorably upon Islam. Nor did his efforts stop here. The period of fasting which he had decreed for the Moslems coincided with that time during which the Hebrews also abstained from food; when Jewish funeral processions passed, the Prophet and his brethren honored them by standing until they had disappeared; and the rite of circumcision—commonly practised by all Arabs out of deference to Abraham, the supposed founder of their holy city, Mecca—was also submitted to by the Moslems to the further pleasure of the Jews, who, however, remained in mystified ignorance as to whether Mohammed himself had undergone that ceremony. It is furthermore likely that the Hebraic horror of Christianity made the Jews look favorably upon this newcomer who, while he might not correspond exactly with the prophet who had been so long and so unsuccessfully anticipated by them, at least appeared to approximate their ideal. What else could be thought of a man who formulated the amazing doctrine that a Jew might synchronously be a devout follower of Abraham and Allah, and might therefore attend both the services of the Mosque and the Synagogue with equal impunity? Indeed, there is much evidence to support the view that, had the Jews saluted Mohammed as *the* prophet who had at last arrived among them, Islam would have been rapidly absorbed by Hebraism.

But Allah had other plans. A year's commingled residence in Medina taught the members of both sects many, many things. Inasmuch as the Jews literally owned the city, the needy Moslems were compelled to turn to them for positions, provisions and for money to borrow; and they soon learnt that their creditors were as merciless as they were devout. Abu Bekr, having approached a certain Pinchas with the quaint request, "Who will lend God a good loan?" was rebuffed with the quick retort, "If God wants a loan, He must be in distressed circumstances"; whereupon Abu, who had absolutely no flair for repartee, won some slight consolation by knocking Pinchas down. The Prophet himself—who, even after he began to extirpate the Hebrews, invariably turned to them when his financial credit was bad—had experiences similar to Abu's; and it is a matter of interest that he now for the first time began to notice that the odors arising from the Jewish habitations were decidedly offensive to his ever-fastidious nose. Another thing that fanned the rising fires of disaffection was the fact that, for more than a year after the Hegira, no Moslem woman gave birth to a child; and the Jews openly bragged that their secret sorceries and enchantments had produced this barrenness. The Moslems, completely upset over this unheard-of catastrophe, exhausted themselves in the attempt to discover an adequate remedy; and the Prophet was so much concerned that he probably composed two Suras especially designed to frustrate the Jewish spells. Yet, in spite of the Hebraic incantations, a Moslem child was born fourteen months after the flight to Medina, and never again was there any doubt as to the fertility of the Moslem women.

The Jews, too, had experienced a mental revolution. A prophet who, as they had discovered, could not speak Hebrew, and who, when put to the test, betrayed an abysmal ignorance concerning the wealth of intricate information stored in the Pentateuch, did not wholly correspond to their idealized conception of their Messiah. They might blandly admit that his dissertations were satisfactory, but when he pressed his prophetic claims upon them they courteously retorted that *their* particular prophet must be able to trace his lineage straight back to David. They objected, also, when they noted how great a proportion of his time Mohammed spent in his harem, whereas the Jews, of all people, might well have regarded that harmless idiosyncrasy as a clinching proof that his mission was divine. Again, when the Prophet vainly tried to save the life of one of his earliest converts by cauterizing his sore throat, the Jews poked fun at him. "If this man were a prophet, could he not have warded off sickness from his friend?" they mockingly asked. And all that Mohammed could think of to say was this: "I have no power from my Lord over even mine own life, or over that of any of my followers. The Lord destroy the Jews that speak thus!" From this time on, instead of sitting up night after night, as he had once done, telling affecting tales about the Children of Israel, he began to belabor their descendants in the pages of the Koran. Where it had once iterated and reiterated the manifold virtues of the ancient Hebrews, it now discussed their manifold vices—their idolatries, backslidings, and betrayals—at even greater length; and an almost Christian fervor breathes from those pages where the Prophet asseverates that the wilful stupidity of the Jews caused them to reject him even as they had previously spurned Jesus.

Some faint-hearted Hebrews, who perhaps suspected what was coming, were diplomatic enough to swallow the new faith entire, thereby winning from Mohamned the appellation of "Witnesses." Abdallah, son of Salam, was a shining example. Having slyly induced his brethren to give him a character testimonial before they knew that he was about to become a renegade, he presented it to the Prophet who was so pleased that he assured Abdallah he was already in Paradise—even Sa'd, chief of the Aus, had not received a comparable congratulation. But Abdallahs among the Jews were rare. Most of them continued to snicker at the hilarious ignorance and bombast revealed in Mohammed's homiletical discourses, to disregard Allah's grim warning that they should repent and turn to Islam "before We deface your countenances, turning the face backwards," and to wax fat on the miseries of the Moslems. On the other hand, the Moslems themselves no longer made any effort to conceal their desire to hold their noses when they were compelled to approach the Jews on business matters; and the Prophet himself shortly decided to put a summary end to all attempts at reconciliation and brotherhood.

Perhaps the success that attended his decision to fight during the sacred months suggested the idea that he was now strong enough to break definitely with the Jews. One day, not long afterward, while he stood at prayer in the Mosque with his face turned as usual toward the Temple of Solomon in Jerusalem, he received a lightning revelation to turn "toward the holy Temple of Mecca. Wheresoever ye be, when ye pray, turn toward the same." The divine injunction came just after he had prostrated himself twice toward Jerusalem; quick as a flash he reversed himself—an action instinctively followed by all the automatons in the audience—and faced toward the south until the service was ended. This symbolic event signalized his determination henceforth to separate himself wholly from the Jews, as well as to gratify the atavistic longings of his zealots who had never quite succeeded in relinquishing their love for the Black Stone and the Kaba; then too, Mohammed had grown very tired of listening to a favorite Hebraic taunt: "This Prophet of yours knew not where to find his Kibla [house of worship] till we pointed it out to him." The Jews, who fully understood the sinister significance of Mohammed's sudden right-about-face, were much perturbed; and they had reason to be, for he lost no time in sundering every tie that connected the worship of Allah with Hebraic ceremonies. He commanded the Moslems to keep their fast before or after the Jewish Day of Atonement; he once more followed the Arabic custom of combing his hair instead of letting it drift loose, as the Jews did; he altered the Moslem funeral rites so that they again corresponded to the immemorial Pagan ritual; and he changed the regulations pertaining to the lunar indisposition of females to a system that Moses asssuredly would not have approved. For it must be demonstrated that Allah was more powerful than Jehovah; that Mohammed, as the last of a long line of prophets, had an ultimate claim upon the sacerdotal office; and that the superior wisdom which the Jews boasted concerning celestial matters over which he had hitherto asserted his sole jurisdiction would be of no use whatever to them —after they were dead.

III

The triumph of Bedr encouraged Mohammed to expedite his plans of revenge against his internal foes; directly or indirectly, he stimulated his accomplices to assassinate them. Peculiarly sensitive as he was to the slurring satires and puns which the Jews had aimed against some of his most cherished speeches, and being wholly incapable of retorting in kind, he was only too pleased when the Moslems showed a demoniacal readiness to avenge his wounded honor with sharper-pointed weapons than epigrams. Asma, a poetess strongly on the side of the Jews, composed some verses that castigated the disaffected Medinese for bowing before an interloper whom she represented as hoping that the city would "be done brown" so that he might enjoy a toothsome banquet; shortly afterward, one of the Prophet's men stole into her room at midnight and, after taking the trouble to remove her nursing baby, thrust his sword through her breast. Next morning Mohammed paused in his prayers at the Mosque long enough to inquire of the murderer, "Hast thou slain the daughter of Merwan?" "Yes," was the reply, "but tell me now, is there cause of apprehension?" "None," the Prophet assured him, "a couple of goats will hardly knock their heads together for it." Then, turning toward the congregation, he shouted: "If ye desire to see a man that hath assisted the Lord and His Prophet, look ye here!" A second satirist, old Abu Afak, a Jewish convert, foolishly attempted to carry on the work begun by Asma. "Who will rid me of this pestilent fellow?" inquired Mohammed; and within a few hours Abu Afak, while carelessly sleeping in a courtyard, was also transfixed with a sword. Both of these deeds were committed within a week after Bedr.

About six months later one Ka'b, another Jewish versifier who, like most satirists of his time, signalized his craft by anointing his hair on one side, allowing his clothes to become disordered, and wearing but one shoe, decided to amuse himself by making public a series of poems that were intimately concerned with the amatory charms of some of the most generous Moslem women. Of a beauty named Um al-Fadl he wrote:

"Of saffron color is she; so full of charms that if thou wert to clasp her, there would be pressed forth Wine, Henna, and Katam;
So slim that her figure, from ankle to shoulder, bends as she desires to stand upright, and cannot.
When we met she caused me to forget my own wife Um Halim, although the cord that bindeth me to her is not to be broken.
I never saw the sun appear by night, except on one dark evening when she came forth unto me in all her splendor."

Ka'b was also believed to be engaged in double dealings with the Koreish, and so the Prophet offered this public prayer: "O Lord, deliver me from the son of Al-Ashraf, in whatever way it seemeth good unto Thee, because of his open sedition and his verses." And lest there might be doubt as to how he wished his supplication to be fulfilled, he asked his servants this pointed question: "Who will ease me of the son of Al-Ashraf? for he troubleth me." Maslama's son Mohammed, a well-known Moslem libertine, responded, "Here am I—I will slay him." "Go!" exclaimed the happy Prophet, "the blessing of God be with you, and assistance from on High!" Aided by four conspirators, this Mohammed succeeded in luring Ka'b away from his bride on a moonlight night. Suddenly seizing his long hair, they pulled him to the ground with the shout: "Slay him! Slay the enemy of God!" and immediately stabbed him to death. "Welcome!" said Mohammed on their return, "for your countenances beam of victory." "And thine also, O Prophet!" they replied, as the victim's head was tossed down before his feet.

On the following day Mohammed, having decided that the only good Jews were dead or exiled ones, gave the Moslems free leave to kill them upon sight. Muheisa, a converted Khazrajite, at once availed himself of this long-desired privilege by slaughtering the first Hebrew he chanced to meet; and when his brother Huweisa chided him for his excessive zealotry, he growled: "By the Lord! if he that commanded me to kill him had commanded to kill thee also, I would have done it." "What!" screamed Huweisa, "wouldst thou have slain thine own brother at Mohammed's bidding?" "Even so," was the cool answer. "Strange indeed!" said the aghast Huweisa, "hath the new religion reached to this? Verily, it is a wonderful faith!" And he immediately proclaimed his own conversion to Islam.

Many of the Jews would doubtless have liked to follow his example, but their day of grace was past; no longer could they qualify as "Witnesses" for Mohammed. For indeed his heart was set upon their extermination, or—what was even better—the robbery of their goods; and to that end, like a good general, he proceeded first against those who dwelt in Medina. About a month after Bedr, he went to the wealthy tribe of Beni Kainuka, who practised the goldsmiths' trade in Medina, and peremptorily announced his errand thus: "By the Lord! ye know full well that I am the Apostle of God. Believe, therefore, before that happen to you which has befallen Koreish!" But they hurled defiance at him, so he decided to wait until he could find a convenient excuse to attack them. He soon found it. As a Moslem girl was trading in a goldsmith's shop one day, a frivolous-minded Jew sought entertainment by creeping up behind her and pinning the bottom of her skirt to her shoulder; howls of merriment followed and the poor maiden almost died of shame. A Moslem who soon avenged the insult by slaying the sprightly Jew was killed in turn by other Jews; and thus the Prophet was conscientiously able to proceed against the Beni Kainuka—for had they not broken the solemn treaty hitherto contracted between the Moslems and the Hebrews? A fortnight's siege ended in their abject surrender; their hands were then tied and they were led out to be executed. At this moment Abdallah ibn Obei, who still retained some remnants of power in Medina, approached the Prophet with a plea for mercy. But the only reply was an averted face, so Abdallah seized Mohammed's arm and repeated his request. "Let me go!" the Prophet angrily screamed; then, since Abdallah still clung to him, he again shouted, "Wretch, let me go!" But Abdallah continued to hang on, begging that pity be shown; and Mohammed, who still feared Abdallah's might, grudgingly commanded, "Let them go!" though he could not refrain from adding, "The Lord curse them, and him too!" So their lives were spared, but their rich possessions were confiscated and they were at once sent into banishment; and Mohammed solaced himself for his Pyrrhic victory by selecting the choicest of their weapons for himself. When Abdallah bitterly reproved one of the Prophet's leading confederates, he was met by the curt response: "Hearts have changed. Islam hath blotted all treaties out."

Such, indeed, was the fact. Within a year the murderer of Ka'b was dispatched to the Jewish tribe of Beni an-Nadir—which was suspected of being in secret league with the Koreish—with this commission: "Thus saith the Prophet of the Lord. Ye shall go forth from out of my land within the space of ten days; whosoever after that remaineth behind shall be put to death." When they protested on the ground that such treatment would be rather severe on a people who had never injured Islam, Mohammed's envoy merely remarked, "Hearts are changed now," and abruptly left them. After prolonged and anxious consultation, they decided to hold fast to their fortress—a proceeding so unusual for their race that, when the Prophet heard of it, he shouted in delight: "Allah Akbar! The Jews are going to fight! Great is the Lord!" His enthusiasm was somewhat dampened, however, when he discovered that a lengthy siege failed to dislodge them; accordingly, he determined to hasten matters by destroying the pick of their palm-trees with fire and axe. They protested that this act was both barbarous and contrary to Mosaic law; and, while Mohammed was no longer much interested in Moses, he well knew that his deed was opposed to the unwritten laws of Arabian warfare. The Koran, therefore, was soon adorned with this exculpatory passage: "That which thou didst cut down of the Date-trees, or left of them standing upon their roots, it was by the command of God, that He might abase the evil-doers." The Beni an-Nadir, in fact, were so completely abased by the relentless siege that they were glad to surrender their lands and go into exile on the generous condition that their lives should be spared.

These episodes relating to the Beni Kainuka and the

Beni an-Nadir are only two of many like illustrations, that might be discussed at wearisome length, which demonstrated two significant facts: Mohammed had succeeded in ridding Medina of its indwelling foes, and he had decided to destroy the Jewish settlements throughout all Arabia. The massacre of the Beni Koreiza followed as a matter of course; and in 628 the last Hebraic stronghold of much account was also dismantled. In the summer of that year Mohammed, heading sixteen hundred men, pounced upon the opulent city of Kheibar, which lay about one hundred miles to the north of Medina—a distance that shows how wide the sweep of the Prophet's victorious arm had reached. The motive which inspired him to assault this people appears to have sprung from the consideration that they had failed to avenge the murder of one of their own tribesmen by a Moslem; for the Prophet may well have believed that such an aggressively peace-loving clan merited the severest punishment. In any case, they were not true believers; and, at this stage of Islam, that fact in itself constituted a more than ample pretext for the opening of hostilities. Kheibar's forts fell in rapid succession before the impetuous rush of the now veteran Moslem army. As Mohammed gaily charged from one conquered stronghold to another, he continually raised the rapturous shout: "Allah Akbar! Great is the Lord! Truly when I light upon the coasts of any People, woe unto them in that day!" After the conquest was complete, Kinana, chieftain of Kheibar, was tortured in the hope that he would reveal his hidden treasure. Fires were burnt upon his breast until he was so nearly dead that he could not have confessed even had he so desired; and Mohammed, who realized that he had carried the thing too far, ordered his head to be chopped off.

Kinana's notoriously beautiful wife, the seventeen-year-old Safiya, and her companion were then fetched up to the Prophet; the companion, seeing the headless trunk, beat her face and howled aloud. "Take that she-devil hence!" snapped Mohammed; but he tenderly folded his mantle around Safiya's head to screen her from the sight, for he had determined to marry her. His approaching nuptials, however, were nearly ruined by Zeinab, a Jewess who had lost all her male relatives and her husband on that fateful day. She poisoned a kid, tastily garnished it, and then placed it before him, smiling and coaxing him to eat. Having distributed the least desirable parts among his fellows, he bit off a choice mouthful from the shoulder; but barely had his teeth closed on it when he cried, "Hold! surely this shoulder hath been poisoned," and indecorously spat it out. One man who had partaken of the meat died, and

Mohammed himself is reputed to have been afflicted with such violent pains that he was repeatedly cupped between the shoulders; yet within a short time he was observed to disappear with the fickle-hearted and coyly reluctant Safiya behind the bridal tent.

Thus the former Meccan merchant and exile passed from conquest to conquest. He was now not only a prophet—plenty of contemporary men professed a similarly exclusive claim to that commonplace title—but the recognized dictator over Medina and an extensive range of contingent territory; furthermore, the terror inspired by the mere mention of his name had penetrated to the most distant stretches of Arabia, and was beginning to arouse sinister forebodings in adjacent nations. Had his relatively unbroken succession of victories made him an inexorably ruthless tyrant whose actions were wholly prompted by an insatiable ambition, or had they but reaffirmed his ceaselessly reiterated claim that he was only plastic clay in Allah's hand? Did he delight to glut himself in wanton bloodshed, or, in the inmost regions of his spirit, did he believe that the punishments meted out upon his enemies had actually been self-inflicted inasmuch as they had refused to accept the one true God? "And He hath caused to descend from their strongholds the Jews. . . . And He struck terror into their hearts. A part ye slaughtered, and a part ye took into captivity. And He hath made you to inherit their land, and their habitations, and their wealth, and a land which ye had not trodden upon; and God is over all things powerful. . . I am the strongest, therefore Allah is with me." Did those exultant words emanate from a profligate, coldly calculating and atrociously barbarous hypocrite, or from a humble and grateful penitent whose sole wish was to be a channel through which Allah's divine purposes might be made manifest? The answer forever bides.

VIII

AVOCATIONS

I

Incessant wars and rumors of wars by no means occupied all of Mohammed's attention. He might be prophet, statesman, general and practically king, but he was also something more: he was a family man on a large scale. Aloof and reserved on public occasions, he was excessively affectionate toward his friends, and indeed some of his wives. Since he no longer had any small children, he was particularly fond of little tots; while standing at prayer he sometimes held a child in his arms, and at Medina he often allowed a little girl to lead him around by the hand. From the plumbless depths of his character a vast and intricate collection of odd mannerisms, which occasionally corresponded with the surpassing dignity of his office, came to the surface; and all the manifold resources of psychology, philosophy and related branches of erudition have been exhausted in the attempt to analyze or synthesize his personality from these *disjecta membra.* But the dry bones still remain scattered and unfleshed; all the prodigal resources of modern scholarship have excavated fewer vital facts about the Prophet than one of his most favored wives or friends might have related in less than a day. When, therefore, they speak with voices whose authenticity is generally granted, they should be allowed to hold the stage.

Ayesha, certainly, was one of them. Questioned once about her illustrious consort, she tartly replied: "He was a man just such as yourselves; he laughed often and smiled much." "But how would he occupy himself at home?" the insistent voice continued. "Even as any of you occupy yourselves," came the abrupt response. "He would mend his clothes, and cobble his shoes. He used to help me in my household duties; but what he did oftenest was to sew. If he had the choice between two matters, he would always choose the easier, so as that no sin accrued therefrom." Ayesha obviously had few illusions about Mohammed; but that is one of the peculiar privileges of great men's wives, and besides he was her senior by more than forty years—a fact that probably accounts very largely for her continual underestimation of his several abilities. Her highly partial record, accordingly, should be corrected and supplemented with equally pertinent particulars.

For indeed, despite his felicity in cobbling, sewing, milking his goats and tarring his camels, there were many things that he did not like at all. He detested lying on the part of others, and separated himself from those of his adherents who cultivated a natural taste for mendacity, until they repented; he held the custom of usury in special abhorrence: "One dirhem of usury which a man eats, knowing it to be so, is more grievous than thirty-six fornications," he declared. He also loathed dogs and pictures—"Angels will not enter a house containing a dog or pictures," and "Every painter will be in hell," he oracularly announced, but the reason for this outburst is obscure. Perhaps it was because Arabian art was notoriously bad—and then again, perhaps he was jealous of anything that, no matter how rude and primitive, was entirely beyond his comprehension. Once, during public prayers, he chanced to notice that his mantle was richly figured, and when he had ended he said: "Take away that mantle, for verily it hath distracted me in my prayers, and bring me a common one"; and on another similar occasion he threw off a silken robe in disgust, saying, "Such stuff it doth not become the pious to wear." He wore a golden ring until he noticed that all the people were beginning to follow his example, whereupon he went into the pulpit, pulled the ring off with the words, "By the Lord I will not wear this ring ever again," and then prohibited the use of such adornments. A friend who had sent him a present in the form of a steaming dinner was much chagrined when it was returned uneaten and even untouched by his fingers—for he "used to eat with his thumb and his two forefingers," and, "after he had finished eating, he licked his blessed fingers: first the middle one, then the prayer-finger, and last the thumb" —but he was pacified when the Prophet explained that he had not tasted it because onions had been cooked with the food; for Gabriel, he went on to say, strenuously objected to the odor of both onions and garlic. Furthermore, he abstained from tasting lizards, for he feared that they were descended, by some inexplicable metempsychosis, from a certain tribe of Israel. He commonly reclined during his meals, though sometimes "he would sit on his left leg, posting up the right; and if he was very hungry, he would sit down altogether and post up both legs."

Yet the catalogue of his likes was far more extensive than the list of his aversions. He was so devoted to everlasting prayers that his legs often became swollen from long standing; and when anyone remonstrated with him, he would reply: "What! Shall I not behave as a thankful servant should?" He was very careful not to yawn during his devotions, and if perforce he sneezed, "he made a moderate noise, covering his blessed face with his robe-sleeve and putting his blessed hand before his nostrils," after which he would ejaculate, "Praise be to Allah!" Before commencing his orisons, he always sniffed up several handfuls of water from his right hand and then blew the liquid out with his left hand. Ordinarily, he prayed with his shoes on, though he once took them off while engaged in public supplication—a deed immediately aped by the entire audience; but the Prophet at once informed them that their action was unnecessary, "for he had merely taken off his own because Gabriel had apprised him that there was some dirty substance attaching to them." His prayers were so earnest and vehement that "it might be known from a distance that he was speaking by the motion of his beard"—which he had let grow until it reached to the middle of his broad chest; but he regularly clipped his moustache. When it was once suggested to him that his appearance would be vastly improved if he reversed the process, the counselor was properly rebuked. "Nay," said Mohammed, "for my Lord hath commanded me to clip the moustaches and allow the beard to grow."

In more mundane matters, too, his tastes were equally pronounced. He affected white clothes chiefly, but was also partial toward red, yellow and green garments, and he sometimes wore woolens. Scrupulously neat in his personal habits, and ever ready to condemn untidiness (yellow teeth, in particular) in his companions, he yet wore a turban, wrapped many times around his head, whose lower edge looked "like the soiled clothes of an oil-dealer." But such carelessness was uncommon, for his clothes, though mostly inexpensive, were habitually clean and neat. When he donned freshly laundered clothes, he was accustomed to remark: "Praise be to the Lord, who hath clothed me with that which shall hide my nakedness and adorn me while I live." He had a perfect mania for toothpicks: at night he invariably kept one handy to use before performing his ablutions; while traveling he always carried a generous supply; indeed, he used them so frequently between his wide-spaced teeth, "white as hailstones," that he gradually wore his gums away; and one person chanced to observe him, toothpick in mouth, making a gurgling, "a-ccha" noise as if he were going to disgorge his food.

The narrowness of his means at Medina limited his gluttonous desires for a time, but his rapid successes soon enabled him to feast upon delectable dainties. He was very fond of sweetmeats, honey, cucumbers and ripe dates ("When he ate fresh dates he would keep such as were bad in his hand") and he eyed the pumpkin with particular favor. One of his servants, gazing abstractedly at some pumpkins one day, after Mohammed's death, was overheard saying "Dear little plant, how the Prophet loved thee!" Like a true Arab, he preferred mutton to all other flesh. "I once slew a kid and dressed it," narrated a Medinan. "The Prophet asked me for the forequarter and I gave it to him. 'Give me another,' he said; and I gave him the second. Then he asked for a third. 'O Prophet!' I replied, 'there are but two forequarters to a kid.' " The meal that he relished with most gusto, however, was "a mess of bread cooked with meat, and a dish of dates dressed with butter and milk." He had a predilection for several wells around Medina whose waters, he said, were both "cold and sweet," and, after he drank, he sometimes bathed in them or invoked a blessing on their contents by spitting into them. Close-fisted and frugal most of the time, he readily loosed his purse-strings when he saw something whose appeal was irresistible. He once paid about twenty camels for a single dress, and also gave eight golden pieces for a mantle. At bedtime he regularly put antimony on his eyelids, "saying that it made the sight more piercing, and caused the hair to grow"; he had a crystal goblet with silver trimmings, a copper vase for his baths, and an ivory comb;

but perhaps his chief fancy inclined toward perfumes. "We always used to know when Mohammed had issued forth from his chamber by the sweet perfume that filled the air,"one of his servants testified. He indulged without stint in musk and ambergris, and he burned camphor on odiferous wood so that he might enjoy the smell. With her customary acumen, Ayesha put the gist of the matter into one pithy sentence when she said: "The Prophet loved three things—women, scents, and food; he had his heart's desire of the first two, but not of the last." In fact, Mohammed himself argued that these two innocuous diversions intensified the ecstasy of his prayers.

II

Mohammed's adoration of particular women was nevertheless tempered with penetrating discretion toward the sex in general. It is true that he abrogated the usage which permitted, and even encouraged, sons to inherit their fathers' wives, and that the code of Islam allowed single ladies to be mistresses of their own actions; but it is also true that married women continued to be treated merely as sports and playthings for the convenience of their husbands. "Men stand above women," says the Koran, "because of the superiority which God hath conferred on one of them over the other. . . . Wherefore let the good Women be obedient. . . . But such as ye may fear disobedience or provocation from, rebuke them, and put them away in separate apartments, and chastise them. But, if they be obedient unto you, seek not against them an excuse for severity; verily God is lofty and great." While Moslem husbands might easily obtain an absolute divorce if they chose, the idea that women might occasionally desire the same privilege seems never to have entered the Prophet's head. Women might win Paradise, to be sure, yet no provision was made whereby they could anticipate such captivating entertainments as were promised to faithful men. Mohammed, in fact, was sagacious enough to entice males to Islam by implying that there would be no occasion for them to lament the loss of their wives in Paradise: "Whenever a woman vexes her husband in this world, his wife among the Houris of Paradise says: 'Do not vex him (May God slay thee!) for he is only a guest with thee He will soon leave thee and come to us' "—and indeed the most subtly cruel punishment that the Prophet ever inflicted upon erring males was to separate them for a period from their wives. If, however, some wives remained refractory in the face of this warning, Mohammed had still another card up his sleeve: "If a man summon his wife to his bed and she refuse to come, so that he spends the night in anger, the angels curse her till morning."

That the Prophet, as was only natural, allowed himself a wider latitude of encounters than was granted to his adherents—who might espouse only four women, but might also form liaisons "without antecedent ceremony or any guarantee of continuance" with any number of female slaves—was made clear by Ayesha. "I was jealous of the women who gave themselves to the apostle of God," she admitted, "and said, 'Does a woman give herself?' Then when God revealed: 'Thou mayst decline for the present whom thou wilt of them, and thou mayst take to thy bed her whom thou wilt, and whomsoever thou shalt long for of those thou shalt have before neglected; and this shall not be a crime in thee.' I said, 'I see your Lord does nothing but hasten to fulfil your desire!'" Yet due allowance should be made for Ayesha's jealousy; for, while Mohammed married approximately twelve women, she was the only virgin among them—the others were widows or divorcees who commonly brought him wealth or desirable political connections. For indeed, though he once playfully chided a Moslem who had married a mature woman instead of a "young damsel, who would have sported with thee, and thou with her," he was too canny to follow his own counsel. At the same time, he preferred women of spirit; in fact, he definitely rejected one girl because "she never cried or complained"—a criticism that certainly could not be aimed against most of his brides.

Khadija was barely under ground when the Prophet prepared to embark boldly upon matrimonial seas. About two months later he married Sauda, a tall, corpulent, mature widow whose brother celebrated the event by sprinkling ashes on his head; he synchronously engaged himself to Abu Bekr's daughter Ayesha, whom he eventually espoused at the age of ten; but it has been suggested that "there may have been something more than ordinarily precocious about the child." She herself attributed her hold on Mohammed's affections not only to her childish beauty, but to her plumpness. "When I was betrothed to the Prophet," she related, "my mother endeavored to make me fat; and she found that with me nothing succeeded so well as gourds and fresh dates. Eating well of them I became round"; yet, as she grew up, she lost her flesh and became thin and willowy. In 624 Omar found himself with Hafsa, a widowed daughter of twenty, upon his hands. Irritated and scandalized by her exhaustive but fruitless endeavors to win a second husband, he offered her in turn to Othman and Abu Bekr, who, knowing that she inherited her father's cranky temper, refused to accept the honor. Omar was so insulted by this double rebuff that he at once flew angrily to Mohammed to make a complaint. The Prophet, at his wit's end because of the social uproar that had been started, saved the situation by marrying Hafsa himself, and thus abundantly gratified his wish to have a wife who cried and complained all the time. Zeinab, widow of one of the heroes of Bedr, became his fifth wife in 626; her gentle and charitable disposition perhaps accounts for the fact that she was the only one of his wives who preceded him to Paradise. His sixth bride was won in a peculiar way. As Abu Selama lay expiring of a wound received at Uhud, Mohammed entered and quieted the wailing women with this prayer: "O Lord! give unto him width and comfort in his grave; lighten his darkness; pardon his sins; and raise up faithful followers from his seed." Just four months later (626), the Prophet pressed his ardent suit upon Abu's widow Um, who, against her better judgment, finally yielded to his importunity.

Meanwhile the much-married man had discovered that his domestic arrangements were getting more and more complicated. Founding a precedent that has since been followed by many Christian churches, he occupied a part of the Mosque. His domestic quarters were established along its eastern wall; they seem to have been constructed from a series of adjacent huts owned by one Haritha, who retired more or less willingly from each of them whenever Mohammed needed a new shelter for a bride; and as the years passed, poor Haritha would barely fix up a new abode before he was shoved out of it. An entrance for the Prophet's exclusive use led from each dwelling into the Mosque; having no separate apartment for himself, he rotated daily from one hut to the other according to a fixed schedule: "the day of Hafsa, the day of Um," *ad finem*. Before long, however, he deliberately infringed upon the rights of all his other wives by breaking the routine in favor of Ayesha—the now lithe and lissom beauty who still toyed with her playthings and frolicked with Mohammed in nursery games—until the deserted wives raised such a squabble that he was forced to emit the famous revelation, so cuttingly commented on by Ayesha, which gave him license to consort with her who pleased him most at the moment.

Conflicting reports have been handed down concerning the acquisition of the Prophet's seventh bride. Going one day to visit his adopted son Zeid, who was absent, he was invited in by Zeid's wife Zeinab, who . . . but here the tales diverge. Some say that Mo-

III

By this time Mohammed had come to be regarded as a highly desirable catch by every widow in Medina, while attractive women came from all the corners of Arabia to offer themselves to the impressionable man. His inordinate masculinity prompted the other Moslems to justify his excess of brides on the judicious ground that his "Excellency had the power of thirty strong men given him"—a consideration that was esteemed by certain discriminating traditionalists to be a proof of what has been characterized as the Prophet's "divinely conferred preëminence." In short, he was every inch a man. His spare, well-moulded figure was tall and commanding; he walked so fast that his gait has been compared to that of a man ascending a hill, or of one "wrenching his foot from a stone," and this rapid locomotion made him unconsciously bend his back until in his last years he became round-shouldered. "That blessed prince's head was large," we are told, "and yet he was not big-headed." His face was lean and rosy, his skin was clear and "soft as woman's," his slightly Roman nose was thin and shapely—some people "might regard his nasal bone as exceedingly long, though in reality it was not so"—his neck, on the unimpeachable authority of Ali, was "like that of a silver urn," and "his blessed mouth was open, but exceedingly graceful." The quality and abundance of his ebon hair has been explained in great detail. Thick and curly masses of it—"not very frizzled or very dangling but just right"—hung about his ears; his vast expanse of beard presumably concealed from vulgar eyes an otherwise conspicuous peculiarity: "from his chest down to the navel there was drawn a thin line of hair, while the other parts of the chest and stomach were hairless, although there was hair on his blessed arms and shoulders and the upper part of his chest." Even in his slumbers he retained his appearance of ease and grace, for he "lay on his right side, putting the palm of his right hand under his right cheek." An admirer summed up his manly comeliness in this poetic outburst: "I saw him at full moon, and he was brighter and more beautiful than she," and another charming tradition affirms that no fly ever alighted on his body. Yet the handsome man was not flawless. The penetrating eyes, fringed with long and lustrous lashes, were red-lidded and bloodshot; ugly gaps disfigured his dazzling white teeth; and on his back was a birthmark which, though held to be the divine "seal of prophecy" that distinguished him as the last of the authentic prophets, was probably a large mole.

Encompassed by six wives and two slave concubines, Mohammed soon discovered that the most energetic efforts were required to provide for their wishes. They not only made a heavy drain on his purse and his larder, but upon his patience; for, while he was rapidly ageing, several of them were just nearing the height of feminine attractiveness, and many youthful Moslems, envious of the conjugal liberties which Mohammed so prodigally claimed, were in the habit of calling at one or another of his houses on matters that had little to do with religion. The favorite, Ayesha, soon got into a scrape that turned his suspicions into open jealousy. She had accompanied him on one of his martial expeditions—a custom of which his other brides frequently availed themselves by the casting of lots, Ayesha being the fortunate winner on this occasion—in a vehicle drawn by a camel and punctiliously veiled from view; and, after he had victoriously returned to Medina and the cart was opened, he discovered to his great horror that she was not inside. When she came up a little later, escorted by young Safwan, she explained that she had lost her necklace, had gone to search for it, and upon her return had found that her guides, thinking that she was inside, had guided the camel and its supposed burden back to Medina. Shortly afterward, she continued, Safwan had chanced to meet her, "expressed surprise at finding one of the Prophet's wives in this predicament," and, upon receiving no reply from the virtuous maiden, had asked her to mount his camel; as she shyly complied, he had averted his face so that he did not see her ascend the beast, and not a word had passed between them on the return journey. No one knows what Mohammed might have done had not scandalous tongues started to wag; but wag they did, and the poor girl, noticing her husband's cold demeanor, promptly fell ill and went to visit her father. The Prophet meanwhile was much disturbed, for the business was very complicated. Should he punish the daughter of Abu Bekr, his most valued and intimate friend, trouble would almost certainly follow; on the other hand, such fellows as Abdallah ibn Obei and the poet Hassan could not be permitted to go around making lewd jokes at his expense. So, visiting Ayesha in the presence of her father and mother, he said: "Ayesha! thou hearest what men have spoken of thee. Fear God. If indeed thou art guilty, then repent toward God, for the Lord accepteth the repentance of His servants." The grief-stricken girl burst out weeping and replied: "By the Lord! I say that I will never repent towards God of that which ye speak of. I am helpless. If I confess, God knoweth that I am not guilty. If I deny, no one believeth me." In this dire predicament, the Prophet fortunately fell into a profound trance; upon his recovery, he wiped great beads of sweat from his brow and exclaimed: "Ayesha! rejoice! Verily, the Lord hath declared thine innocence." "Embrace thine husband!" cried Abu's wife, but Ayesha contented herself with the ejaculation, "Praise be to the Lord!"—in Whom she apparently recognized a capacity for chivalry that was foreign to her husband. And one night not long afterward, hoping perhaps to turn the tables on him, she secretly followed him when he slipped quietly out of the house on what seemed to be an amorous expedition; but she was grievously disappointed upon discovering that he was bent upon no more exciting errand than going to a graveyard to offer up prayers for the dead.

Thus the affair ended. Mohammed, however, immediately improvised a law that imposed a severe scourging upon scandal-mongers who failed to produce four witnesses to substantiate any charge of whoredom —a penalty that was at once inflicted upon Hassan, another man named Mistah, and even one of the Prophet's sisters-in-law; but he dared not treat Abdallah ibn Obei thus. Hassan, moreover, had already been badly wounded by the indignant Safwan; and so Mohammed, who really loved the incorrigibly mischievous versifier, salved his double hurts by presenting him a costly piece of property and a concubine. The grateful fellow immediately manufactured new stanzas in praise of Ayesha's purity, her pert humor, and her supple figure —a series of compliments to which she had the bad grace to retort that the poet himself was disgustingly fat.

Nor did Mohammed stop here; he quickly proceeded to bring about other equally desirable reforms. The institution of the Veil for women—a custom, already not unknown, whose origin was probably due to the common superstitious fear of the horrific "evil eye"—was now imposed upon his harem; and the Koran also made it clear that the day of Moslem peeping Toms was over. "O ye believers! Enter not the apartments of the Prophet, except ye be called to sup with him, without waiting his convenient time. . . And stay not for familiar converse; for verily that giveth uneasiness to the Prophet. It shameth him to say this unto you; but verily God is not ashamed of the Truth. And when ye ask anything of the Prophet's wives, ask it of them from behind a curtain; this will be more pure for your hearts and for their hearts. It is not fitting that ye should give uneasiness to the Apostle of God, nor that ye should marry his Wives after him for ever. Verily that would be a grievous thing in the sight of God. . . The Prophet is nearer unto the Believers than their own souls, and his Wives are their Mothers." All Moslem women, furthermore, were commanded to veil themselves, at home or while walking abroad, from the prying eyes of everyone except a rich variety of relatives. "And say to the believing women that they cast down their looks and guard their private parts and display not their ornaments except what appears thereof, and let them wear their head-coverings over their bosoms, and not display their ornaments except to their husbands or their fathers, or the fathers of their husbands, or their sons, or the sons of their husbands, or their brothers, or their brothers' sons, or their sisters' sons, or their women, or those whom their right hands possess, or the male servants not having need (of women), or the children who have not attained knowledge of what is hidden of women . . . and turn to Allah, O Believers! so that you may be successful."

IV

Yet somehow or other, despite all his efforts to do Allah's will, the Prophet's wives still continued to be rebellious and even fractious. Sadly unmindful of her recent misadventure, Ayesha in particular continued to be as saucy and impudent as ever. When in her distress she had gone to her parents, Ali, who next to Abu Bekr was Mohammed's bosom friend, had consoled him in this way: "O Prophet! there is no lack of women, and thou canst without difficulty supply her place." Upon hearing of this, Ayesha took a temporary revenge by shouting in Mohammed's very face that he liked Ali better than her own father, and a permanent one by treating Ali like a dog for the rest of his life. It chanced, however, that Abu Bekr overheard his vixenish daughter thus berating her husband; utterly unmoved by the fact that she had been standing up for him, Abu at once rushed in and roared, "I will not hear thee lift thy voice against the apostle of God!" But when he seized her and lifted his hand to slap her face, Mohammed interfered; so Abu went away in a foaming rage, while the Prophet heaped coals of fire on Ayesha's head with the comment, "You see how I delivered you from the man." Abu continued to growl and grumble for several days, but eventually returned to find the pair completely reconciled. "Include me in your peace as you included me in your quarrel!" he begged; and Mohammed joyfully answered, "We do, we do!" But perhaps Ayesha provoked the Prophet most of all by failing to treat his religious views with proper decorum; when she was particularly miffed about something, she showed her disrespect by refusing to address him as the "Apostle of God." Once he unwisely told her that, on the day of judgment, all mankind would be raised in the same condition as they had been born—naked, barefooted and uncircumcised. She immediately interrupted his disquisition with the remark that, if this were so, immodest thoughts would prevail, and all that he could think of to say in reply to her untimely jest was that "the business of the day would be too weighty and serious to allow them the making use of that liberty." With an even more lamentable lack of judgment, he once commented on his great love for Khadija—an indiscretion that brought the swift retort: "Was she not old? Has not God given you a better in her place?" "No, by God!" exclaimed the homesick man, "there can never be a better! She believed in me, when men despised me; she relieved my wants, when I was poor and persecuted by the world."

Besides Ayesha's shrewishness, too, he was forced to endure mean tricks used by some of his other pestering wives, who, knowing his strong aversion to such smells as onion and garlic, sometimes took pains to eat malodorous foods. In his perplexity he devised various avenues of escape; but even the horse-races and the performances of singing-girls, which he not infrequently included in his list of pleasures, afforded him little lasting relief. There was some solace, however, in the fact that many of his famous followers were also stung by domestic broils. Abu Bekr and Omar, coming one day to visit the Prophet, found him gloomy and glum in the midst of his family. After Omar had made the aside remark, "I must say something to make the Prophet laugh," he began thus: "O Apostle of God, if I see Bint Kharija [his wife] asking me for money I get up and throttle her!" Mohammed, immensely tickled in spite of himself, replied, "These women about me, as you see, are asking for money." Abu Bekr immediately bounded up and started to choke Ayesha; Omar also seized his daughter Hafsa by the throat and savagely demanded, "Will you ask the Apostle of God for what he does not possess?"—upon which both women simultaneously gasped, "By God, we will never ask him for anything he does not possess!" This incident seems to have taught Mohammed how to manage his women better. Having first absented himself from their ministrations for about a month, he appeared with a new string of commandments. "O Prophet, say unto thy Wives—If ye seek after this present Life and the fashion thereof, come, I will make provision for you and dismiss you with a fair dismission. But if ye seek after God and His Apostle, and the Life to come, then verily God hath prepared for the excellent amongst you a great reward. O ye Wives of the Prophet! if any amongst you should be guilty of incontinence, the punishment shall be doubled unto her twofold; and that were easy with God. . . Ye are not as other women. . . And abide within your houses; and array not yourselves as ye used to do in the bygone days of ignorance. And observe the times of Prayer; and give Alms; and obey God and His Apostle."

After this the air cleared somewhat, so that Mohammed enjoyed a temporary peace; yet it was not long before he incontinently got himself into another scrape. His harem had not particularly objected when he took four other brides in fairly rapid succession—Juweiriya and Safiya, both captives taken in war; Um Habiba, the daughter, *mirabile dictu,* of Abu Sufyan; and the beauteous Meimuna, the sister-in-law of his uncle Al-Abbas, —but when his wives discovered that one of his latest concubines, Mary the Coptic maid, was about to become a mother, confusion was worse confounded. For they knew that, above all else, Mohammed desired a son: he had no living boy, he was naturally affectionate, and he suffered agonies from his enemies who applied to him the sobriquet "al-abtar," which means one without descendants, or, translated literally, "one whose tail has been cut off." When in the course of time Mary gave birth to a son, who was named Ibrahim, she was raised from the status of a slave to a position almost on par with her "Sisters"; and Mohammed, overjoyed at his long frustrated good fortune, immediately shaved his head—which had been shorn about a month before—weighed the snippings, and distributed among the poor a corresponding weight of silver. He was also foolish enough to carry his little son to Ayesha and to burst out, in the fulness of parental pride, "Look, what a likeness it is to me!" "I do not see it," snapped Ayesha. "What!" he cried, "canst thou not see the likeness, and how fair and fat he is?" "Yes, and so would be any other child that drank as much milk as he," was the answer.

Not long afterward he was even more imprudent. Hafsa, chancing one day to find the Prophet and Mary in her own particular apartment, lashed out her ever ready tongue at him, and promised that she would tell all his other wives without delay. Mohammed, frightened even more than he had ever been on a battlefield, humbly prayed her to keep quiet and agreed to leave Mary for good; but Hafsa, utterly unable to keep such a flagrant breach of domestic etiquette to herself, at once told Ayesha who of course promptly informed all the other "Sisters." The Prophet, discovering that home life was now absolutely unendurable, once more went into retirement for about a month. He was comforted in his seclusion by both Mary and Allah, one of whom suggested that this passage should be added to the Koran: "Maybe, his Lord, if he divorce you, will give him in your place wives better than you, submissive, faithful, obedient, penitent, adorers, fasters, virgins." But this threat of wholesale divorce does not appear to have worried the enraged women so much as it did their relatives; Abu Bekr and Omar, for instance, were much upset upon learning that their chief should have deserted their daughters in favor of an ex-slave concubine. At this juncture Gabriel luckily appeared on the scene; he informed Mohammed that Hafsa, after all, was a fairly good woman and advised him to take her back. Thus, in fact, the breach was healed; but impartiality necessitates the inclusion of a statement by Mohammed's most adequate modern defender, who swears that the whole episode was an "absolutely false and malicious" invention of the Prophet's enemies. He goes on to say that the passage in the Koran which deals with the affair actually refers to Mohammed's fondness for honey: Hafsa and Ayesha persuaded him to forego it; but then "came the thought that he was making something unlawful in which there was nothing unlawful, simply to please his wives." Thus the Prophet, it is to be inferred, thought that honey was more precious than ten legal brides.

In any case, harmony was restored. Mohammed, worn and haggard from his domestic tribulations, was soon restored to health and amused himself by watching the antics of his growing boy. But when Ibrahim was yet hardly able to toddle around, he began to pine away. Just before his decease, the Prophet clasped him in his arms and sobbed bitterly; when the other watchers endeavored to console him by recalling his own strong objection to the outward expression of grief, he replied in a broken voice: "Nay, it is not this that I forbade, but wailing and fulsome laudation of the dead. . . . We grieve for the child: the eye runneth down with tears, and the heart swelleth inwardly; yet we say not aught that would offend our Lord. Ibrahim! O Ibrahim!" For the child had died while his father was talking, and, after making the observation, "The remainder of the days of his nursing shall be fulfilled in Paradise," Mohammed tenderly comforted Mary. Speechless and heavy-eyed, he kept a steadfast guard while the body was washed and laid out; then he prayed over it and finally followed the procession to the little grave. After it had been filled with earth, he sprinkled fresh water upon the mound and spoke these words: "When ye do this thing, do it carefully, for it giveth ease to the afflicted heart. It cannot injure the dead, neither can it profit him; but it giveth comfort to the living."

IX

THE TRIUMPHANT RETURN

I

Six long years, with their burden of foreign and domestic struggles, had elapsed since the Hegira; yet the recollections of Mecca, the Kaba, the Black Stone—in short, the memories of *home*—had remained ineradicably fixed in the minds of the Prophet and his flock. About half of Arabia, and approximately three-fourths of his wives, might now be pretty well under his dominion; but his heart often troubled him when he recalled his sins of omission in failing to fulfil the Lesser and Greater Pilgrimages—and, incidentally, the hateful truth that the intransigent Koreish still ruled the beloved city. Why, therefore, should he not undertake a pilgrimage during one of the sacred months? for surely, the mere fact that he himself had previously violated their sanctity could not rightly be held against him if he returned as a humble penitent. The Koreish, bound by adamant Arabian custom, would almost certainly allow him and his followers to make their sacrifices to the national religion; and, even in case his ancient foes should molest the journeying Moslems, perhaps—*perhaps*—he would be able to deal with them.

In a dream he imagined himself and his worshiping band going through the stiff ritual of pilgrimage: encircling the Kaba, slaughtering the sacrificial victims, and completing the other well-remembered ceremonies. The Moslems, after listening to his fervid narration of this vision, pulsated with desire to accompany him; and so, having taken a bath and donned the two-piece pilgrim garb, in February, 628, he set out, mounted on Al-Kaswa, at the head of some fifteen hundred votaries each of whom was armed with a sword, a bow and a quiver of arrows. At one stage of the journey they halted and, uttering the plaintive cry "Labbeik! Labbeik! (Here am I, O Lord! Here am I!)," placed their curious ornaments around the necks of seventy votive camels. In the busy midst of these pious engagements, however, the Prophet did not neglect to dispatch a spy to report on the behavior of the Koreish; the envoy finally returned with the news that the Meccans were obviously distrustful of Mohammed's peacefully religious intentions, and that, in very truth, a large body of armed Koreish was guarding the road that led to Mecca. "Their wives and little ones are with them," said the spy, "and they have sworn to die rather than let thee pass," adding the further detail that they were clothed in panthers' skins—a symbol of their determination to fight like beasts in an effort to bar any advance. Mohammed and his people therefore decided to continue toward Mecca by a sinuous route that would lead them to the edge of the sacred city. At this juncture Al-Kaswa stopped short and refused to budge another inch. "She is weary," the Moslems insisted; but the Prophet replied: "Nay, Al-Kaswa is not weary; but the same hand restraineth her as aforetime held back the elephant"—for, as became a loyal Arab, he had not forgotten how Arabia had been saved from the invader Abraha. He further declared that he would not march upon the city, for fear that the few Moslems who were still living there might chance to be harmed in the struggle that might take place; but it is also possible that he checked his advance because he had learnt that the Koreish, hearing of his own manœuver, had also deviated in such a way that they still blocked his path.

Very soon afterward, a Koreishite deputation approached to interview Mohammed. "I have no other design but to perform the pilgrimage of the Holy House," he insisted, "and whosoever hindereth us therefrom, we shall fight against them." This sally was met by the retort that the desperate Meccans "will not suffer this rabble of thine to approach the city." A long, wrangling dispute followed in which blows came near being struck; and the only concession that the Prophet could obtain was the information that "this year he must go back; but in the year following he may come, and having entered Mecca then perform the pilgrimage." Mohammed, who realized that his acquiescence to these instructions would irreparably harm his prestige, decided to send a counter delegation to Mecca. Omar was the first man requested to act in this capacity; but that fearless fighter begged off on the plea that he had no powerful relatives in the city to protect him against the Koreish, and, pointing to Othman—whose slight to Hafsa had not been forgotten—suggested that *he* be the Moslem representative. Othman had excused himself from fighting at Bedr on the grounds that his wife, the Prophet's own daughter, was ill; but, realizing that the influence of his family connections would protect him on this occasion, he readily consented to depart. His return was so long delayed that Mohammed feared he might have been treacherously slain, and a tensely dramatic scene took place. The Prophet, standing beneath an acacia tree and encircled by the entire number of his votaries, requested a solemn pledge that they would not turn their backs, but, if necessary, would fight till the last man dropped; the covenant was individually sealed as each man clasped Mohammed's outstretched hand—when Othman suddenly appeared, entirely unharmed. Nevertheless, the Prophet was immensely pleased; indeed, he never ceased to refer to this auspicious event, which had symbolized the strength of the union of religious ecstasy and martial enthusiasm that dominated his willing slaves.

A treaty of peace was eventually drawn up. For ten years the Koreish caravans were to be unmolested, and during this same period extraneous clans could be converted either to Islam or to the faith—such as it was —of Mecca; in the following year, also, the Moslems were to be allowed to complete their pilgrimage, but this year they must return unedified and still burdened with their sins. Perhaps Mohammed swallowed this bitter medicine the more readily because previous experience had taught him that treaties were mere scraps of paper; yet he found it excessively irritating to endure the high-handed methods of the noted orator Suheil, ambassador for the Koreish. The Prophet, assuming as a matter of course that he himself should phrase the language of the covenant, began to dictate to Ali, who willingly served as a scribe, in this high-flown manner: "In the name of God, most gracious and merciful"—"Stop!" Suheil abruptly interrupted, "as for God, we know Him; but this new name, we know it not. Say, as we have always said, *In thy name, O God!*" "In thy name, O God," Mohammed repeated, "These are the conditions of peace between Mohammed the Prophet of God and"—"Stop again!" commanded the imperturbable spokesman. "If thou wert what thou sayest, I had not taken up arms against thee. Write, as the custom is, thine own name and thy father's name." "Write, then," said the amazed but ever tactful Prophet, "between Mohammed son of Abdallah, and Suheil son of Amr . . ." and so on until the end. The document was then duly witnessed by members of both factions; and Mohammed, firmly resolved to perform at least a modicum of his vows, shaved his head (or cut his hair; historians have not determined the facts about the matter), and, while all the Moslems treated their heads in a similar manner, he directed that the doomed camels should be sacrificed.

The unexpected outcome of this journey left many Moslems unsatisfied. Some of them—both the "Shavers" and the "Cutters"—had refused to part with their hair until the Prophet ordered them to do so; Omar, in particular, had so completely recovered the strength of his trembling knees that he threatened to head a renegade movement. Obviously, therefore, it was high time to produce a new message from on high. Even before the return journey was begun, the words "Inspiration hath descended on him" were eagerly repeated throughout the encampment, and a great crowd collected around the Prophet, who, standing upright on Al-Kaswa's broad back, began to intone thus: "Verily, We have given unto thee an evident Victory," adding, at the end of a tediously prolix mass of jubilantly phrased but wholly unintelligible rhetoric: "Now hath God verified unto His Apostle the Vision in truth; ye shall surely enter the Holy Temple, if it please God, in security, having your heads shaven and your hair cut. Fear ye not; for He knoweth that which ye know not." As he concluded, one of the onlookers exclaimed, "What! is *this* the Victory?" "Yes," came the calm reply, "by Him in whose hand is my breath, it is a Victory." And in fact, despite the Prophet's muddy-mindedness on this occasion, there was much to justify his statement. Perhaps he realized that the peaceful outcome of his pompous expedition, which was certain to be noised over a large part of Arabia, would win him more converts than force had ever done—for had he not convinced the Koreish of his pacific intentions, and had *they* not treated him with high honor? Thus, indeed, it turned out; various tribes, hoodwinked by highly colored accounts of the pilgrimage, at once sought to make alliances with Mohammed; and the result was that, during the next year, Islam grew as it had never grown before.

Two interesting incidents took place soon after Mohammed had returned to Medina. Abu Basir, a youthful acolyte of Islam who still lived in Mecca, became so restless under the domination of the Koreish that, after a series of bold assaults and hairbreadth escapes, he managed to reach Medina in safety; the Prophet was so much stirred by the lad's tale of rash but admirable bravery that he commented, as if speaking to himself: "What a kindler of war, if he had but with him a body of adherents!" Abu Basir, encouraged by these words, at once organized a band of seventy similarly inclined young braves who, for the next few months, assaulted Koreishite caravans and killed the captives with so much gusto that Mohammed, at the humble request of the Meccans, finally felt constrained to command the robbers to cease from kindling war. The second event was of an entirely different sort. Some of the Medinese Jews, who had openly and loudly proclaimed their adherence to Islam, surreptitiously obtained several of the Prophet's blessed hairs, and, after tying them into eleven knots around the branch of a palm-tree, lowered the evil invention into a well. Their sly and malignant design was soon rewarded: Mohammed grew feeble, his mind became afflicted with stranger hallucinations than ever before, he neglected his devotions, and he even showed indifference toward his wives. But Gabriel shortly revealed the cause of his malady; the well was examined, the necromantic knots were loosed, and the Prophet, thus freed from the voodooistic spell, experienced a lively recrudescence of his manifold talents.

The time finally drew near when, according to the terms of the treaty, the Koreish were to evacuate Mecca for three days so that the Moslems might perform their pilgrimage in peace. On this occasion about two thousand zealots accompanied Mohammed, and, although each one was restricted by treaty to carry only a sword, a large amount of armor was taken along, while the travelers were also preceded by a considerable force of cavalry. As the procession approached the holy city, the Koreish obediently withdrew and, stationed on the surrounding hills, kept a wary eye on the curious scenes that followed. The eager devotees, upon viewing the deeply revered Kaba again for the first time in seven years, raised the now almost joyous ululation, "Labbeik! Labbeik!" Mohammed, astride Al-Kaswa as usual, neared the Kaba, gently touched the Black Stone with his staff, and—apparently still mounted on Al-Kaswa—went seven times around the sacred temple. His absorption in these reverent pursuits, however, did not cause him to forget more important concerns: at his special bidding, the Moslems footraced around the Kaba three times at top speed, to demonstrate to the observant Koreish that they were in excellent physical condition; then, at a somewhat slower pace, they circled the building four times more.

Three days were occupied in fulfilling the remaining rites; yet the Prophet, who, through the aid of Al-Kaswa, had kept himself fresher than his foot-sore compatriots, and who had meanwhile taken the opportunity to engage himself to Meimuna, continued to tarry in apparent forgetfulness of his sworn promise to leave the city on the third day. He was brought rudely to his senses on the morning of the fourth day, when two leaders of the Koreish came abruptly up and said: "The period allowed thee hath elapsed; depart now therefore from amongst us." "And what harm if ye allowed me to stay a little longer," Mohammed graciously inquired, "celebrate my nuptials in your midst, and make for the guests a feast at which ye too might all sit down?" "Nay," was the harsh answer, "of any food of thine we have no need. Withdraw from hence!" To disobey was to invite an immediate war; and inasmuch as the Prophet was not yet ready for the struggle that, in his heart of hearts, he had long anticipated, he directed that an immediate departure be made—a stipulation that compelled him to content himself with the consummation of his nuptials at a spot about ten miles from Mecca.

But, despite its somewhat inglorious conclusion, the

grandiose adventure accomplished several things of much importance. In a general way, Mohammed benefited from the fact that the Koreish had not failed to be impressed by the dignified yet ominous Moslemite display of religious and warlike ardor. With their own eyes, they had seen what an exalted rank the renegade Prophet had attained among his servile henchmen; they had noted, too, the instantaneous and unquestioning obedience with which his least desire had been met. He profited, also, in that the deepest instincts of his confederates had been aroused at the renewed visitation of the familiar and unforgettable scenes of those happy, bygone days when they had dwelt in peace and moderate prosperity at Mecca, until the implacable requirements of Islam had wrenched them from their cherished moorings. Once again they had been irresistibly compelled to realize that they were but outcasts and wanderers, to whom Medina had never grown really congenial, and who now poignantly reflected that Mecca, and Mecca alone, was home. In particular, the Prophet gained two notable converts to Islam: Khalid, who had commanded the cavalry that brought about the Moslem defeat at Uhud, and Amr—who was equally versatile in poetry, diplomacy, and military strategy—were so impressed by Mohammed's magnificent gesture in conducting the Moslems to Mecca that they decided to desert the vacillating Koreish and cast their fortunes with the progressive cause of Islam. Under the Caliphs who succeeded the Prophet, the intrepid Khalid—divinely protected by some of Mohammed's hair which he wore in his cap as a charm against misfortune—won such imperial victories that he acquired the title "The Sword of Allah"; and the sagacious counsels of Amr also won him a high place in the annals of Islam. Furthermore, the accession of these two was not without its immediate effect. They were straws that showed how the wind was veering: the Koreish had not only failed to recover the prestige they had dropped at Bedr, and to benefit by the Moslem debacle at Uhud, but they had lost the confidence of some of their outstanding men of action. The time was swiftly approaching when the rankling stigma of Uhud would be blotted out, when the Prophet would take a final and complete revenge on his life-long enemies, and when the Meccans would treat Allah with an even more touching reverence than they already bestowed upon Al-Ozza, Hubal, the Kaba and the Black Stone.

II

A serious reverse suffered by the army of Islam postponed the inevitable surrender of Mecca for a year.

One of Mohammed's emissaries, sent with a message urging a certain Syrian leader to join Islam, had been murdered by another Syrian chieftain; and the Prophet, presumably ignorant that an attack on Syria was equivalent to a declaration of war against the Roman Empire itself, immediately sent a force of three thousand Moslems to avenge the crime. As the soldiers departed, he invoked this blessing on their errand: "The Lord shield you from every evil, and bring you back in peace, laden with spoil!" He then privately gave Zeid the permission to make treaties in his own name, instead of in the name of Mohammed himself, in order that the covenants might the more readily be broken.

But once again Allah proved to be either absent-minded or very inconsiderate. As the Moslem soldiers neared the Dead Sea, they were amazed to learn that an enormous army, skilled in Roman methods of battle, was waiting to crush them. Conflicting counsels were offered; many wished to instruct the Prophet of this ill news and await his subsequent advice; but Abdallah ibn Rawaha roused the wilting courage of his fellows with these ringing words: "What have we marched thus far but for this? Is it in our numbers, or in the help of the Lord, that we put our trust? Victory or the martyr's crown, one or other, is secure. *Then forward!*" His maniacal frenzy was imparted to his companions, who, meeting the powerful Roman phalanx at Muta close to the Red Sea, madly threw themselves upon the foe. Mohammed's life-long friend Zeid, who had most unwillingly relinquished Zeinab in favor of the Prophet, bravely bore the white Moslem banner until he willingly relinquished his life for Islam. Jafar, another Moslem hero, then seized the inspiring piece of cloth and, shouting out: "Paradise! O Paradise! how fair a resting-place! Cold is the water there, and sweet the shade," was shortly able to test the truth of his pæan. Abdallah ibn Rawaha then fell in turn, bearing the flag to the ground with him; at this moment Khalid demonstrated the genuineness of his recent conversion by rallying the terrorized Moslems and immediately speeding toward Medina with the fragments of the army.

The Medinese, deeply dismayed at the rout, found some relief by hurling dust and jeering taunts at the truants; but Mohammed put a stop to their meanness in this fashion: "Nay, these are not runaways; they are men who will yet again return to battle, if the Lord will." Struck to the heart by the loss of so many tried companions, he first went to Jafar's house, where, clasping the dead man's children in his arms, he sobbed bitterly; departing thence to the home of Zeid, he broke down completely when Zeid's little daughter threw herself tearfully into his arms. "Why thus, O Prophet?" asked one person, who inconveniently recalled Mohammed's many injunctions that Moslems should not display their sorrow at the times of death. "This is not forbidden grief," was the response, "it is but the fond yearning in the heart of friend for friend." Yet next morning, as he worshiped in the Mosque, he smiled and remarked: "That which ye saw in me yesterday was because of sorrow for the slaughter of my Companions, until I saw them in Paradise, seated as brethren, opposite one another, upon couches. And in some I perceived marks, as it were wounds of the sword. And I saw Jafar as an angel with two wings, covered with blood—his limbs stained therewith."

Though smiles wreathed his face, a mordant desire for vengeance gnawed at his heart. What a tragedy that the Syrian tribes, who of late had been deeply impressed by the conquest of Kheibar, should have learnt that Islam, after all, was not invulnerable! Amr, the recent Meccan turncoat, was accordingly placed in command of a Moslem expedition to Syria, where his strong right arm succeeded in restoring the Prophet's weakened prestige; yet the setback at Muta still rankled in the minds of the Medinese, and Mohammed was probably keen enough to realize that the situation could be remedied only by the achievement of some extraordinary, astounding, unparalleled coup. No longer would he insist that defeats were moral victories; no longer would he indite Suras that placed the burden of defeat squarely upon Allah's broad shoulders; no longer would he seek advice from Abu Bekr or his other intimate counselors in martial concerns. Mecca, Mecca! *There* lay the answer to all the questions that vexed his dreams. All that was needed to justify the taking the holy city was some specious pretext. So, at any rate, certain historians argue and they may well be right; yet Mohammed was driven by such intricate and inexplorable motives that one does well to hesitate before placing his finger on this or that spot in his journey and saying, "Such and such an idea impelled him to act thus at this particular point." It is conceivable, for example, that, by a mental process not wholly unfamiliar to moderns, he may have been influenced in his subsequent action by the belief—natural enough, surely, for an Arab!—that Mecca was Allah's own country.

In any event, a reason for attacking Mecca was soon found. The Khozaa, a tribe in the neighborhood of the sacred city, had chosen under the provisions of the treaty between Islam and Mecca to join the Moslem cause; another adjacent clan, the Beni Bekr, that contrariwise had gone over to the Koreish, had proceeded, with the assistance of some disguised Koreishites, to attack the Khozaa who of course hurried to Mohammed for redress. Here, at last, was the long deferred opportunity. The spokesmen of Khozaa had barely finished the tale of their wrongs when the happy Prophet, who was only half clothed, bounded to his feet and made this fervent promise: "If I help you not in like wise as if the wrong were mine own, then let me never more be helped by the Lord! See ye not yonder cloud? As the rain now poureth from it, even so shall help descend upon you speedily from above." When the Koreish heard of this affair, their perturbation was so great that they dispatched Abu Sufyan to see if it were possible to obtain a renewal and extension of the treaty; but Abu, the diplomat, turned out to be no more successful than Abu, the general. Upon arriving at Medina, he went straight to his daughter, Um Habiba, wife of the Prophet; but, as he started to seat himself on her carpet, she drew it away from him. "My daughter!" he remonstrated, "whether is it that thou thinkest the carpet is too good for me, or that I am too good for the carpet?" "Nay, but it is the carpet of the Prophet, and I choose not that thou, an impure idolator, shouldst sit upon the Prophet's carpet," she coldly answered. "Truly, my daughter, thou art changed for the worse since thou leftest me," Abu sighed; then, stepping out of doors in front of the Mosque, he loudly cried:

"Hearken unto me, ye people! Peace and protection I guarantee for all." Mohammed, who was standing near by, thereupon interrupted to remark, "It is thou that sayest this, not we, O Abu Sufyan!" At this point Abu decided that it was time for him to return home.

Mohammed rapidly and secretly laid his plans. He requested many allied tribes to join with him, meanwhile withholding his ulterior intentions from them; and not until the very moment of the departure did he enlighten the Medinese—at which time he also warned them, by this prayer, to keep the secret from the Koreish: "O Lord! Let not any spy carry tidings to Koreish; blind their eyes and take their sight away until I come suddenly upon them and seize them unawares!" On January 1, 630, the largest Moslem army ever collected thus far—with the additions of the desert allies, it numbered close to ten thousand—set out for Mecca. Al-Abbas, the shifty time-server, who had assisted his nephew-Prophet in his escape from Mecca ten years earlier only to be compelled to pay a large ransom for himself after Bedr, now decided once and for all that it would be highly advisable to espouse the Moslem cause; so he slipped out of Mecca on the sly and, approaching the Prophet, was much gratified upon being welcomed with outstretched arms.

Mecca, however, was destined to be saved from violent assault, though the precise reason for this happy conclusion is not known. Concerning the event that follows, it is not clear whether Abu Sufyan acted for himself alone, or at the bidding of his Koreishite companions. One night, as ten thousand Moslem campfires illuminated the heavens from the hills that encircled Mecca, Abu Sufyan came gliding toward the tent of Mohammed, where he was commanded to remain away until morning. Returning at that time, he was thus accosted by the Prophet: "Out upon thee, Abu Sufyan! hast thou not yet discovered that there is no God but the Lord alone?" "Noble and generous Sire! Had there been any God beside, verily he had been of some avail to me," whined Abu. "And dost thou not acknowledge that I am the Prophet of the Lord?" catechized Mohammed. "Noble Sire! As to this thing, there is yet in my heart some hesitancy," replied the trembling but truthful fellow, who probably found it difficult to look upon his own son-in-law as the direct agent of God. At this moment Al-Abbas boldly intruded with these well-chosen words: "Woe is thee! it is no time for hesitancy, this. Believe and testify forthwith the creed of Islam, or else thy neck shall be in danger!" Then Abu diplomatically capitulated, and vehemently proclaimed that he did indeed believe there was no God but the Lord alone and that Mohammed was His Prophet; and Mohammed, who had scored what was probably the greatest individual triumph of his career, joyfully exclaimed: "Haste thee to Mecca! haste thee to the city; no one that taketh refuge in the house of Abu Sufyan shall be harmed this day. And hearken! speak unto the people, that whosoever closeth the door of his house, the inmates thereof shall be in safety." Then, closely escorted by Al-Abbas, Abu went forth, pausing a moment, as his amazed eyes swept the innumerable warriors around him, to remark, "Truly this kingdom of thy nephew's is a mighty kingdom." "Nay, Abu Sufyan!" chided Al-Abbas, "he is more than a king—he is a mighty Prophet!" "Yes, thou sayest truly; now let me go," replied Abu as he edged away. Arriving home, he promptly repeated the Prophet's message; and never before, in all her long and distinguished history, had Mecca witnessed such a scurrying of feet and banging—or draping—of doors as followed.

When the Moslem and allied hosts came victoriously parading through the deserted streets, only one conflict occurred. The impetuous Khalid, whose force was greeted by a flight of arrows from a small band of bitter-enders, was so delighted at his unexpected good fortune that he followed up the assault until twenty-eight of the foolhardy fugitives had been slain. The

Prophet, standing on an eminence, was surveying with sparkling eyes the fair scene stretched out before him when he chanced to see this sporadic fray. "What! did I not strictly command that there should be no fighting?" he shouted in his anger; but when Khalid's just grievance was made clear, he calmed down and commented, "That which the Lord decreeth is the best." Then, descending into the city on Al-Kaswa's back, he once more touched the Black Stone politely with his staff and urged the patient camel seven times around the Kaba. Pointing at the idols which surrounded its walls, he ordered that they should at once be overthrown—indeed, tradition affirms that, as he aimed his staff at each image, it immediately tumbled down on its face—and shouted out one passage that he happened to remember from the Koran: "Truth hath come, and falsehood gone; for falsehood verily vanisheth away." He next entered the holy edifice, devoutly prostrated himself, and then stood watching with delighted eyes the labors of Omar, who, by means of a cloth wetted in Zemzem, rubbed out the pictures of such idols as had been painted on the walls. Then Mohammed gave back the key of the temple to its hereditary guardian, and, turning to Al-Abbas, thus addressed him: "And thou Al-Abbas, I confirm thee in the giving drink from out of the well Zemzem to the pilgrims;

it is no mean office this that I give now unto thee"; and nevermore did the already opulent double-dealer entertain the least doubt as to the justice of his nephew's cause. Bilal, commanded by the Prophet, immediately ascended the Kaba and sounded the call to prayer; the subservient multitude knelt and worshiped, though a few among them could not refrain from expressing, in very subdued tones, their disgust at being obliged to obey a negro slave. The Prophet next issued this proclamation: "Whoever believeth in God, and in the day of Judgment, let him not leave in his house any image whatever that he doth not break in pieces." Now, since the Arabians in general cherished the belief that a capable god should be able to defend himself, the easy demolition of the deities in the Kaba had convinced the Meccans that their gods—even Al-Ozza and Hubal—were as useless as so many dolls. And so, while the destruction of the helpless icons was enthusiastically carried out in every Meccan home—while Abu Sufyan's wife, Hind, smashed her favorite god as energetically as she had once ripped Hamza's vitals out, and further insulted the deity by the charge that it had vilely cheated her all her life—Mohammed, fatigued and dusty, retired to a corner of his tent and, as his daughter, Fatima, shielded him with a screen, gave himself a thorough bath.

It is more than probable that the Koreish were immensely relieved and pleased with the quiet and almost bloodless subjugation of their city. In truth, although some of them became sycophants who cringed and fawned in order to win Mohammed's good will, the majority doubtless took pride in the fact that their prodigal son, whose magnetic name was beginning to cause apprehension even beyond the borders of Arabia, had returned to demand his fatted calf. Their slumbers need never more be broken by nightmares of his precipitate assault upon them; further, the tiresome burden of ruling, or trying to rule, for the welfare of Mecca was now transferred to his gracious and omnipotent hand. As a religious but non-political capital, moreover, Mecca would be secure from whatever might betide in the shifting destinies of time. And they were right. Mohammed had won so easily, he had reached such an unapproachable eminence, that he could afford—it matters little whether from scrupulous policy or wholly unselfish generosity—to be magnanimous. If he directed the death of four ingrate Meccans, he proclaimed a general amnesty for all the rest; if he cast out idolatry, he substituted a religious ritualism which coalesced the leading dogmas of the various Meccan sects; and if he temporarily ruined Meccan commerce by his famously unscientific monkeying with the calculation of time—inasmuch as the pilgrimage months no longer always coincided with the period when caravan trade flourished—he bountifully blessed her with a permanent revenue that, after thirteen hundred years, still continues to pour into her coffers. For, as Islam has continued to prosper, all devout Moslems have at one time or another journeyed from every quarter of the globe to visit that "Navel of the Islamic faith" which seems to them to be the earthly replica of that indescribably glorious Paradise which awaits the faithful; and myriads of curious, and even irreverent, sightseers have perennially flocked thither to enjoy the endless diversion afforded by one of the greatest religious entertainments on the globe.

X

MOHAMMED AND ALLAH

I

THE time rapidly approached when the Prophet was to renounce the multitudinous burdens and joys of his earthly existence, and depart to that supernal haven which he had so frequently and so eloquently depicted. For Allah, who had not gazed upon his faithful servant since the episode of the midnight journey, yearned to clasp him forever to his breast; and Mohammed believed that Khadija, the Virgin Mary, Potiphar's wife, and Kulthum, sister of Moses, longingly anticipated his arrival; so too, though for very different reasons, did Gabriel, who desired a respite from his enervating trips between Paradise and Medina. But a few months more were yet to be granted Mohammed—months that were to exemplify the same indomitable energy, the same assiduous zealotry, that he had manifested for the last twenty years.

Mecca was now irrevocably sealed to Islam; but that very fact caused fearful apprehension among those Bedouin peoples who were yet idolistic and untamed. The powerful Hawazin and Beni Thakif tribes, who occupied an extensive territory southeast of Mecca, decided that they had a fair chance to crush the arrogant dominion of this would-be conqueror of all Arabia while he was yet rejoicing in his easy conquest of the holy city; and to that end they assembled about six thousand men. Mohammed, on learning of their plans, determined to nip this insurrection in the bud, and quickly departed at the head of twelve thousand seasoned troops; so imposingly spectacular was this great force that Abu Bekr could not restrain his admiration. "We shall not this day be worsted by reason of the smallness of our numbers!" he gleefully shouted, and the Prophet smiled in agreement. Then, seated on a white mule, he followed in the rear of the soldiers.

As the Moslem troops were defiling through a narrow pass in the valley of Honein, the ambushed foe suddenly charged upon them with such impetuosity that they first hesitated, then recoiled and fled in utter panic. "Whither away?" shouted Mohammed, while the broken columns sped by him. "The Prophet of the Lord is here! Return! return!" But his lungs were unequal to the emergency, so he bade Al-Abbas try the strength of his voice; and his uncle used his stentorian oratory to such good effect that it rose above the clamorous turmoil of retreat. A number of the penitent fighters came shamefacedly back, and, shouting out, "Ya Labbeik! Here we are, ready at thy call!" stopped the flight of the rest and turned to face the pursuing Bedouins. Mohammed, gazing at the bloody spectacle from the safety of an adjacent hill, was so overpowered with warlike ardor that he screamed: "Now is the furnace heated; I am the Prophet that lieth not; the seed of Abd al-Muttalib!" Then, hurling a fistful of gravel at the foe, he continued: "Ruin seize them I swear they are discomfited. By the Lord of the Kaba, they yield! God hath cast fear into their hearts." The hard-won victory was indeed so complete that thousands of prisoners, forty thousand sheep and goats, and four thousand ounces of silver were seized as spoil. And the Prophet, repenting of his self-confidence before the battle, indited a Sura which stated that the preliminary defeat had been caused by over-confidence in numbers, and that success had come only because God "sent down Hosts which ye saw not, and thereby punished the Unbelievers."

Yet he realized that, in order to clinch the victory, it would be imperative to capture the Bedouin stronghold at At-Taif. In assaulting that place he trusted, in addition to the heavenly hosts, to the most modern Byzantine inventions of warfare—the testudo and the catapult. But they both proved to be ineffective, for the simple reason that the besieged garrison destroyed the wooden testudo by hurling molten metal upon it, thus making it impossible to use the catapult at all. As the weary weeks dragged on, Mohammed endeavored to expedite the surrender of the fort by destroying the vineyards around At-Taif and offering freedom to any slaves who would desert the stronghold; but even these traditional devices proved to be useless, and, warned by a dream that the heavenly will was not in favor of continuing the siege, he decided to accept the counsels of his assistants, who were also getting very tired of the business. The Prophet then withdrew to the place where the booty won at Honein had been stored.

Now it happened that the worldly wise members of the Hawazin, having had plenty of time to reflect upon the matter, had decided that by embracing Islam they might get off with a lesser punishment than would otherwise be the case. Mohammed, of course, was much pleased to welcome them to the faith; but when they suggested that, inasmuch as they were now loyal Moslems, both their property and their prisoners should be returned to them, he was wholly unable to concur. Instead, he gave them this choice: "Whether of the two, your families or your property, is the dearer to you?" Impaled on the horns of this dilemma, they were forced to admit that their relatives were more precious, and the prisoners were accordingly set free. The Prophet was so much pleased by the possibilities of this barter and trade in the name of Islam that he offered one hundred camels to Malik, chief of the Hawazin, if he too would embrace the Moslem cause; and Malik, being a wise and prudent man, speedily accepted the terms. But some of the other people, fearing that they were to lose the loot as well as the prisoners, rushed up to Mohammed and, shouting aloud, "Distribute to us the spoil, the camels and the flocks!" treated him so roughly that his mantle was ripped from him, whereupon he sought to save himself by backing against a tree. "Return to me my mantle, O Man!" he cried, "return the mantle; for I swear by the Lord that if the sheep and the camels were as many as the trees of the forest in number, I would divide them all amongst you." Since they still continued to press him, he held up a hair and exclaimed: "Even to a hair like this, I would keep back nought but the fifth; and even that," he hastily decided to add, "I will divide amongst you."

Thus the mob was quieted and the Prophet soon made good his word; in fact, so generous was he in dealing presents out among his new auxiliaries that he sometimes gave a double gift to those who insisted that they deserved it. Spectacles such as these could not fail to anger many of his veteran associates who had received nothing at all; never before had they met with such cavalier treatment as this. When one of them made the direct charge that Mohammed was unfair, he was met with the irate reply: "Out upon thee! If justice and equity be not with me, where will ye find them?" The Prophet furthermore stated that, so far as the elder Moslems were concerned, faith was its own reward—a saying which the Medinese, who had waxed fat and rich on the plunder of so many conquests, found very hard to swallow. They continued to show their displeasure so long that Mohammed finally called them together and spoke honeyed words. "Ye men of Medina, it hath been reported to me that ye are disconcerted, because I have given unto these Chiefs largesses, and have given nothing unto you. Now speak unto me. Did I not come unto you whilst ye were wandering, and the Lord gave you the right direction? needy, and He enriched you; at enmity among yourselves, and He hath filled your hearts with love and unity?" As murmurs of assent began to rise, he continued: "Why are ye disturbed in mind because of the things of this life wherewith I have sought to incline these men unto the faith in which ye are already stablished? Are ye not satisfied that others should have the flocks and herds, while ye carry back with you the Prophet of the Lord? Nay, I will never leave you. If all mankind went one way, and the men of Medina another way, verily I would go the way of the men of Medina. The Lord be favorable unto them, and bless them, and their sons and their sons' sons for ever!" Then, weeping until the tears streamed down their manly beards, his confederates shouted in unison, "Yea, we are well satisfied, O Prophet, with our lot!" However, lest any doubt might remain in the minds of any, Allah Himself speedily revealed that alms—for both taxes and war-plunder were thus ingenuously disguised—were intended, among other persons, "for them whose hearts are to be gained over. . . . It is an ordinance from God; and God is knowing and wise." Thus, by timely revelations, the faith of Islam was steadily increased; the most devout Moslems, indeed, regarded the inexorable duty of paying onerous financial tributes to Allah as an inestimable privilege; though it is true that a few hard-hearted wretches publicly proclaimed that each successive addition to the Koran furnished them new cause for amusement.

II

Honein was the last of a series of victories that laid the Koreishite ghost forever; the Prophet was now virtually the ruler of the entire Arabian peninsula; and, having made a triumphant entrance into Medina, he proceeded to execute a project that had long been dear to his heart. As early as the year 627, he had sent out feelers to a branch of the empire of Byzantium on the subject of conversion to Islam; his envoy on that occasion, though courteously welcomed and given a special dress of honor, had accomplished little. But now, while embassies from numerous Arabian tribes made haste to present themselves to him, hoping to make a good bargain by trading their recreant idols for the all-conquering Allah, Mohammed's apparently chimerical fancy to extend Islam in, and even beyond, the bounds of the Roman Empire was again aroused. The lonely visionary of Mount Hira, the Meccan outcast, risen to the imperial position of temporal and spiritual dictator of all Arabia, vibrated with the insatiable desire to make Islam dominant over the world. *He* might not live to see that glorious fulfilment; yet perhaps his notorious gift of prophecy enabled him to pierce the veil that shadowed the future: the advance of Islam under successive Caliphates until its haughty realm extended from India to the western limits of Spain—the stemming of the onrushing Saracen tide by Charles Martel at Tours—the wayfaring Crusaders bent upon rescuing the Holy Land from Mohammedan dominion—the revival of interest in classic lore which was the direct result of the Crusades—the concomitant Renaissance of learning and of Christianity until Christian warriors, with a Bible in one hand and a sword in the other, supplanted the imperial Crescent with the even more imperial Cross—the Cross that has itself become associated with imperialism. Thus, by a grotesque chain of closely linked events, Mohammed might—had his prophetic eye been gifted with sufficient range—have envisaged himself in the odd position of being the chief instrument in the world-wide promulgation of classicism and of Christianity. For, had the Middle Age Crusaders not been inspired with unremitting zeal to wrest the Holy Grail from Islam, there might well have been no Renaissance, no stimulation of mental and spiritual activities, and, consequently, no such Christian imperialism as now holds so much of the world under its righteous sway.

Had Mohammed foreseen all this, however, he might possibly have had less interest in those embassies to and from his house in the Mosque, where, sprawling on his mat and cooling his face with a palm-leaf fan, he issued his endless commands and listened to endless requests from suppliants. Indeed, his office work had become so voluminous that he now made use of an amanuensis, Zeid the son of Thabit, who was specially skilled in the Hebrew and Syriac languages. Though quick-witted and agile of tongue, Zeid was inclined to be so forgetful and generally scatter-brained that the Prophet was obliged to tell him to thrust his pen behind his ear, "for this will bring to remembrance that which the distracted mind is seeking after."

If tradition may be trusted, Mohammed was not always over-successful in his dealings with prospective converts. The Christian tribe of Nejran, in central Arabia, came to him after an ostentatious exhibition of prayer in the Mosque, and loudly declared that they were Moslems; but the Prophet, observing that they wore silk-lined clothes—which he particularly detested, though it is true that he ordered such hapless Moslems as became afflicted with the itch or "louse-disease" to wear silken shirts—rightly doubted their sincerity and merely turned up his nose at them; they therefore departed and shortly returned in monastic garb. Their leader, doubtless inspired with the hope that a display of knowledge on his part would gain them better terms, offered to debate with Mohammed concerning the mystical nature of Christ, but he wisely declined to comply and stated that he would prefer to engage in a cursing contest; and in fact, while one of his most uncritical admirers affirmed that the worst oath he ever used was "May his forehead be darkened with mud!" the Koran, among other authentic documents, furnishes considerable evidence to the contrary. Realizing that they would be no match for him in such an ordeal, the Nejranites capitulated to the extent of agreeing to pay tribute, though they refused to acknowledge his divine mission; the Prophet acceded to this compromise, but soothed his ruffled dignity by declaring that they were one of the two worst tribes in all Arabia, and by announcing that Christians, as well as Jews, were to act as substitutes for Moslems in Hell-fire. Moreover, believing that Christianity and Judaism were both on their last legs, he devised the humane stipulation that, provided Christians and Hebrews submitted to the earthly rule of Islam and paid "tribute with their hands," they would be permitted to profess whatever faith they chose. Yet he would presumably have been better pleased had all Arabians manifested the delicate concern shown by a fellow named Al-Jarud. "O Prophet," said he, "I have hitherto followed the Christian faith, and I am now called on to change it. Wilt thou be *Surety* for me in the matter of my religion?" "Yea, I am thy surety that God hath guided thee to a better faith than it," Mohammed gladly answered.

Two dispatches were probably sent to Heraclius, Emperor of Byzantium, who had just completed a victorious struggle with Persia. The first one, which requested him to cease the idolatrous worship of Jesus and His Mother, to reverence the one true God, and to recognize the mission of Mohammed, was apparently disregarded; a second message, couched in like terms, prompted a vassal of Heraclius to request permission to punish the insolent pretender who sent it, but Heraclius forbade any needless expedition against the contemptible person who had audaciously signed himself "Mohammed the Apostle of God." The King of Persia, on receiving a similar note, merely tore it up; and the Prophet, on hearing of this outrage, prayed aloud: "Even thus, O Lord! rend thou his kingdom from him!" It may be presumed that neither Heraclius nor the Persian King even suspected that, within a decade or two, their mighty empires would be paying tribute to Islam. A letter that Mohammed sent to Ruayyah, of Suhaim, was treated more respectfully than the one that had been dispatched to the Persian monarch; for Ruayyah used it to mend a hole in his water-skin. Another powerful chief, having listened to Mohammed's delegate, instructed him to carry back this message: "How excellent is that Revelation to which thou invitest me, and how beautiful! Know that I am the Poet of my tribe, and an Orator. The Arabs revere my dignity. Grant unto me, therefore, a share in the rule, and I will follow thee." The Prophet, on being informed of this, snarled: "Had this man asked of me but an unripe date, as his share in the land, I would not have given it. Let him perish, and his vainglory with him!"—and it is confidently stated that the presumptuous snob did, in fact, die within a year. The Roman Governor of Egypt, too, refused to endorse Mohammed's claims—"I am aware," he said, "that a prophet is yet to arise; but I am of opinion that he will appear in Syria"—yet he atoned for his stubbornness of heart by sending Mohammed a double present in the form of a white mule and a black concubine.

Mohammed, meanwhile, was showing his interest in his recent converts by altering their Pagan names to titles that better suited his almost feminine fondness for daintily euphemistic words. For example, "Zeid of the Stud" right gladly abandoned his plebeian appellation when he was rechristened "Zeid of the Good"; "the Wolf, son of the Cub," was similarly glorified by becoming "Allah's Servant"; and an "Oppressor" suffered a welcome sea-change into a "Well-doer." But when a tribe called the "Sons of Bastardy" were politely accosted as the "Sons of Chastity," they announced their steadfast desire to remain true to their ancient heritage.

Nor did Mohammed's reforms stop here. The Koran had already prohibited the use of wine; for, years earlier, the Prophet, while attempting to chide his uncle, Hamza, who was riotously drunk, had received the tipsy response, "Are you not my father's slave?" Liquor, therefore, had been proscribed as a foe to Islam and the dignity of the prophetic office; this rule was so rigorously enforced, in truth, that even a hero of Bedr had been beaten again and again for perennial intoxication, and on one occasion Mohammed himself hurled clods of dirt at another offender. Gambling, too—the casting of lots and the "arrow-game," in which camels were the prizes—had been divinely banned as abominations "from amongst the works of Satan." Mohammed's acutely sensitive nature now led him to proscribe anything that savored of torture inflicted on animals: living birds might not be used as targets in shooting contests; camels were not to be tied up and left to die on their owners' graves; cattle were not to be blinded to avert the evil eye; droughts were not to be broken by the common process of affixing flaming torches to the tails of cattle; horses were not to lose their manes and tails, and asses were no longer to be branded or hit in the face. So scrupulously fastidious was the Prophet that he once ordered some Moslems to stop burning an ant-hill, and he also strongly disapproved the ubiquitous practice of cursing camels and cocks.

His humanity and foresight were also manifested in more important matters. Blood-feuds—the time-honored and almost ineradicable system of tribal revenge for homicide—he endeavored, with partial success, to wipe out by emphasizing the brotherhood of Islam, and by advocating the acceptance of money as a partial compensation: ethical and legislative essays that gradually led to a saner and more peaceful system of government. Whatever may be thought of his general attitude toward women, he certainly benefited them incalculably by setting up laws that enabled them to inherit and hold property; and the luridly overemphasized harem system, Pagan though it may be, has some virtues that are perhaps absent from the Occidental system of prostitution. His advocacy of the custom by which the wives of captives automatically became the concubines of Moslem conquerors has especially irritated certain modern moralists, who apparently have not reflected very deeply on certain canons of contemporary conduct, in which wealth and social distinction play the rôle of the victorious Islamites. He accepted slavery as a matter of course—and, indeed, Islam has never indulged in any foolish civil strife over the question of bondage—but he insisted that slaves must be treated with the utmost kindness. Men who beat their slaves were placed by him among the lowest of the low; he stated that manumission was a pious act, and he sometimes let offenders off from any punishment when they agreed to free their serfs—in short, the present industrial system has little to boast of in comparison with Mohammed's attitude toward serfdom. One other inhuman custom—the ancient practice of female infanticide—was summarily abolished by him; and a tale survives that well illustrates the horror he felt concerning such deeds. Two men, about to yield themselves to the claims of Islam, chanced to question the Prophet about his views on child-murder. "Our mother Muleika was full of good deeds and charity; but she buried a little daughter alive. What is her condition now?" they inquired. "The burier and the buried both in hell," replied Mohammed, upon which his guests became very angry and started to leave. "Come back," he requested, "mine own mother, too, is there with yours." But even this inducement failed to convince them, and so they returned into the outer darkness.

III

Old age, meanwhile, crept gently though inexorably upon the Prophet; but its stealthy approach seemed only to quicken the strength of his arm and the matchless fertility of his intellect. His groveling acolytes, completely bewitched by the magical power of his colossal personality, had exalted him to such a dazzling deification that, had Allah Himself chosen to appear in the streets of Medina, He might easily have passed unnoticed amid the encomiums that were daily showered upon His Apostle—or, rather, Allah might carelessly have been classified with the famous Three Pretenders who, by their conjuring tricks and fake miracles, excited the wrathful amusement of the Prophet in the last year of his earthly life. In fact, it has been pointed out as a matter for deep regret that, while the Koran allows Allah only ninety-nine separate and distinct appellations, His Prophet, at the zenith of his career, was addressed by no fewer than two hundred and one individual titles, including a round score of those that had been applied to Allah Himself.

In the autumn of the year 630, Mohammed conducted his final military expedition. Setting out at the head of a Moslem army that seems to have totaled nearly thirty thousand men, he planned to chastise a Byzantine force that was reputed to have gathered on the Syrian border near Tebuk; but when that place was reached, it was found that there was no Byzantine or any other force to be conquered. Mohammed, thus finding himself in much the same position as the French King in the doggerel ballad, proceeded to march home again after exacting pledges of conversion and immense booty from contingent tribes. His followers, who stated their belief that the "wars for religion now are ended," foolishly began to sell their weapons; but the far-sighted Prophet sternly stopped them and uttered the fateful remark: "There shall not cease from the midst of my people a party engaged in fighting for the truth, until Antichrist appear." Scarcely had he returned to Medina when his heart was gladdened by two events: the death of his only important rival, Abdallah ibn Obei—to whom the Prophet deemed it safe and expedient to pay tribute by following his bier and praying at his grave—and the surrender of At-Taif, the single stronghold that had ever successfully defied his might. He was so exhilarated by the downfall of this fort, indeed, that he let its defenders off from the necessity of breaking their own idols, and, in their stead, elected two Moslems to perform the peculiarly pleasant task.

But perhaps Mohammed most enjoyed the multitudinous activities inherent in his position as a kind and fatherly counselor of his people. The matters which he was besought to adjudicate were extraordinary in their range. One day his prayers would be requested by some prospective bridegroom, who hoped, by the aid of such divine sorcery, to win a wife of unusual goodness and humility; next day he would be begged to specify the precise hour when the world was destined to end; another day would find him busily laying down oracles governing the proper boiling of meat. Only two types of interrogation were taboo: matters that were wholly rational or wholly metaphysical; and Mohammed probably barred these topics on the sensible grounds that preceding prophets who had tampered with either of them had almost uniformly come to grief. Thus it came about that countless apothegms, whose absolute authenticity can never be nicely determined, were confidently claimed to be the children of his brain. Yet, despite the fact that most of these sayings betray a hard-headed and close-fisted sagacity, he was in debt when he died; and perhaps, therefore, the stories concerning his senile delight in the children of his body deserve more credence. Sonless though he was, he could partially console himself by playing with his grandsons, Al-Hasan and Al-Hosein, the progeny of Ali and Fatima, and by reflecting on the transcendent heritage that awaited them as male descendants of himself. In fact, legends sprang up that made a Moslem holy family out of Mohammed, the two boys, and their mother, Fatima, who was further honored by being entitled "The Lady of Paradise"; but, unfortunately for his beatific visions concerning Al-Hasan and Al-Hosein —who frequently entertained themselves by clambering upon their grandfather's broad back while he was bowed in prayer—they turned out to be scurvy fellows who excelled only in incompetence and cowardice.

It may be that Mohammed had a premonition of his imminent death. He decided, at all events, to make a "Farewell Pilgrimage" to Mecca in March, 632, so that he might for the last time feast his eyes on that sacred citadel and undergo the solemn rites of the Greater Pilgrimage—a thing he had not done since the Hegira. He first took a careful bath, then mounted Al-Kaswa, and, accompanied by his entire harem and one hundred votive camels, set forth on the long journey. Having meticulously and painfully performed the prescribed gyrations and genuflections, he cast some small stones at the "Devil's corner"—a spot near Mecca where Abraham was reputed to have met and conquered Satan—and concluded his toilsome duties by delivering a notable speech. After making many additions to, and revisions upon, the already numberless regulations which he had been formulating for more than twenty years, he concluded with these words: "Verily, I have fulfilled my mission. I have left that amongst you—a plain command, the Book of God, and manifest Ordinances—which, if ye hold fast, ye shall never go astray." Then, turning his eyes heavenward, he exclaimed: "O Lord! I have delivered my message and discharged my Ministry." "Yea," came the deep-throated voice of the throng that hemmed him in, "yea, verily thou hast." "O Lord!" he continued, unmindful of the pious interruption, "I beseech Thee bear Thou witness unto it." Returning straightway to Mecca, he encircled the Kaba seven times; thence he went to Zemzem and, having drunk part of the contents of a pitcher filled with its holy water, he rinsed his mouth and asked that the water still remaining in the vessel should be poured back into the well. After abiding three more days at Mecca, he departed from it forever and ambled by easy stages back to Medina.

IV

By this time the sinister tokens of physical decay, unavoidably betrayed by the Prophet, filled everyone with deepest concern. Abu Bekr observed him one day, stroking his beard and looking intently at it; then Abu, his eyes filling with sudden tears, broke out: "Ah, thou, for whom I would sacrifice father and mother, white hairs are hastening upon thee!" "Yes," came the slow response, "it is the travail of inspiration that hath done this. The Suras Hud, and the Inevitable, and the Striking, with their fellows, these have made white my hair." Yet when he actually became ill with pleurisy, or some sort of fever, he named a definite source for the malady: the poisoned mutton which Zeinab, the Jewess, had fed him. "This, verily, is the effect of that which I ate at Kheibar," he declared. "The artery in my back feeleth as though it would just now burst asunder." If his theory was correct, he doubtless died —as his worshipers fervently claimed—the honorable death of a martyr; but it seems probable that his illness had some more tangible origin. Believing that water could not be contaminated, he sometimes carelessly drank from a cistern that was used for slops; as a medicine man who had often attempted to cure his people by charms, cauterization and cupping, he had submitted himself to these practices so frequently that his system must have been gradually weakened; furthermore, Ayesha stated that his health had been poor for years, and that she had constantly dosed him with a profusion of odd concoctions which she herself compounded from innumerable prescriptions recommended by sympathizing friends.

It is not strange, therefore, that, shortly after he had presented a banner to a Moslem army which he commanded to march toward Syria on May 27, 632, for the purpose of avenging the defeat at Muta, he found himself curiously listless and weak. Late one subsequent night, accompanied only by a servant, he stole out to the cemetery on the edge of Medina. After a long and melancholy period of meditation, he thus apostrophized the souls of the dead: "Verily, both ye and I have received fulfilment of that which our Lord did promise us. Blessed are ye! for your lot is better than the lot of those that are left behind. Temptation and trial approach like portions of a dark night that follow one upon another, each darker than that preceding it. O Lord! have mercy upon them that lie buried here!" Next morning, as he passed Ayesha's chamber, he heard her calling out, "My head!—O, my head!" Entering, he gently reproved her thus: "Nay, Ayesha, it is rather I that have need to cry *My head, my head!* But wouldst thou not," he continued, in a feeble attempt to be humorous, "desire to be taken whilst I am yet alive; so that I might pray over thee, and wrapping thee, Ayesha, in thy winding-sheet, myself commit thee to the grave?" Then, in spite of her pain, she railed at him. "Ah, that, I see, is what thou wishest for! Truly, I can behold thee, when all was over, returning straightway hither, and sporting with a new beauty in my chamber here!" But, perceiving that he was really ailing, she forgot her own headache and tenderly cared for him.

Multitudes of conflicting stories have been handed down concerning the happenings of the week that preceded his dissolution; but, inasmuch as they emanated from three distinct political groups, each of whom wished to be recognized as the sole source of truth, the precise occurrences of that fateful period will never be accurately known. At the beginning of his illness it appears certain that, on account of his predilection for baths, he commanded his wives to drench him in cold water on the intriguing theory that, since fever was caused by sparks of Hell-fire, it could be summarily squelched by water; but in this case the douche seems to have had the unfortunate result of sending him into convulsions. It is claimed that, during an interval of temporary relief, he went forth and addressed his devotees in the Mosque—a proceeding which, if it was true, was presumably the reason for his consequent relapse. By Saturday, June 6, his temperature is said to have been so high that Omar, having placed his hand on the tormented man's forehead, quickly withdrew it with the consoling exclamation, "O Prophet, how fierce is the fever upon thee!" "Yea, verily," Mohammed gasped, "but I have been during the night season repeating in praise of the Lord seventy Suras, and among them the seven long ones"; and a moment later he added, "Just as this affliction prevaileth now against me, even so shall my reward hereafter be." On Sunday he was delirious much of the time and suffered such excruciating pain that, following a consultation among his wives, it was decided to administer physic; so they forced the drug down his throat, but, notwithstanding his agony, he readily recognized the too familiar noxious taste and bitterly reproached them. When they admitted their guilt, he cried: "Out upon you! this is a remedy for pleurisy . . . an evil disease is it which the Lord will not let attack me. Now shall ye all of you within this chamber partake of the same. Let not one remain without being physiked, even as ye have physiked me, excepting only my uncle, Al-Abbas." The repentant women immediately arose, and each obediently gave the drug to the other until all had swallowed some of it; and this strange scene around the Prophet's deathbed is one of the small number that are best authenticated.

Certain other tales may be accepted without too much over-scrupulous demur. As he lay alternately drawing the bed-clothes over his face and then tossing them off, he would shriek out unconnected sentences: "The Lord destroy the Jews and Christians! . . O Lord, let not my tomb be ever an object of worship! . . Verily the chiefest among you all for love and devotion to me is Abu Bekr. If I were to choose a bosom friend it would be he; but Islam hath made a closer brotherhood amongst us . . . O my soul! Why seekest thou refuge elsewhere than in God alone? . . Fetch me hither pen and ink, that I may make for you a writing which shall hinder you from going astray for ever." On Monday he seemed a little better, but it was only the final flicker of the dying candle. Toward midday, as Ayesha sat holding his head tenderly on her bosom "between her lungs and her neck," she noticed that his wandering eye had fixed upon a green toothpick; and, after chewing it so that it might be more pliable, she offered it to the dying man who used it for a moment with all his old vigor. But he soon began to sink rapidly, and, as though realizing the imminence of death, he called aloud: "O Lord, I beseech thee assist me in the agonies of death!" Then, while he spasmodically blew breath over his burning body, he thrice repeated, "Gabriel, come close unto me!" It is a regrettable fact that the interesting question of his final utterance must forever remain undecided. One authority declares that he expressed a wish to have concubines treated with consideration; but it is perhaps more appropriate to accept the story that, as consciousness slowly departed, he gently breathed: "Lord, grant me pardon; and join me to the blessed companionship on high. Eternity in Paradise! . . . Pardon! . . . The blessed companionship on high! . . ."—his head fell lower, a cold drop of moisture trickled down upon Ayesha's breast, and all was over.

Yet no one, not even Ayesha, could believe it for a

time. Thinking that he had only fainted, she called aloud for help; and Omar, who immediately came in, looked lovingly upon the familiar and still lifelike features and exclaimed: "The Prophet is not dead; he hath but swooned away." But Abu Bekr, who was welcomed into the sacred adytum with the feminine salutation, "Come, for this day no permission needeth to be asked," at once realized the awful truth, which he cautiously made known by stooping and kissing his master's face, and saying: "Sweet wast thou in life, and sweet thou art in death. Yes, thou *art* dead! Alas, my friend, my chosen one!" After kissing the face a second time, he covered it with a striped cloth and gently withdrew from the room, while Mohammed's wives beat their faces, uttered loud and plaintive ululations, "and there arose a wailing of celestial voices." The corpse was washed and laid out, and, in addition to the garment which he wore at the time of his death, two sheets of costly white linen were wrapped around it. After some discussion, it was decided on the advice of Islam's new leader, Abu Bekr—"I have heard it from the lips of Mohammed himself," he announced, "that in whatsoever spot a prophet dieth, there also should he be buried"—that a deep grave should be excavated beneath the apartment of Ayesha. During the night the ominous thud of pickaxes disturbed the troubled dreams of the Prophet's widows—"I did not believe that Mohammed was really dead," confessed Um Selama, "till I heard the sound of the pickaxes at the digging of the grave, from the next room"—and next day a constant stream of weeping Moslems filed by to look for the last time upon the beloved face that now resembled a sheet of withered parchment. That evening the body was lowered into the grave, whose bottom had been covered with the Prophet's precious red mantle; the gaping hole was built over with unbaked bricks, plain earth was then shoveled upon the tomb, and there, in the august simplicity of his domestic abode, Mohammed's form has ever since remained.

Meanwhile—since all things are possible with Allah—it may surely be conjectured that Gabriel had abundantly granted the Prophet's dying request, and had borne him, along the familiar route previously traversed in the midnight journey from Jerusalem, for the second and last time into the presence of his Maker. And there—may not one hope?—at the zenith of the Seventh Heaven, in that ravishing Paradise which so closely resembles an infinitely idealized Arabian oasis, he abides even unto this day and will continue to dwell "For ever therein—a fair abode and resting place!"—enjoying the ineffable entertainments that have been prepared for the Moslem saints and martyrs who, triumphant over sin and suffering, have been welcomed to the indepictable felicities of the divine beatitudes; quaffing deep draughts from those inexhaustible "rivers of wine" which the Koran promises to those who have manfully abstained from all earthly elixirs; continually cherished by seventy dark-eyed, deep-bosomed Houris who, as befits inhabitants of the "Garden of Delight," individually reside within the modest seclusion of enormous hollow pearls; ever and anon chanting, through his black-bearded lips, the ninety-nine beautiful names of Allah, and concluding with the inevitable refrain, *"La ilaha illa Allah, Mohammed rasul Allah!"*

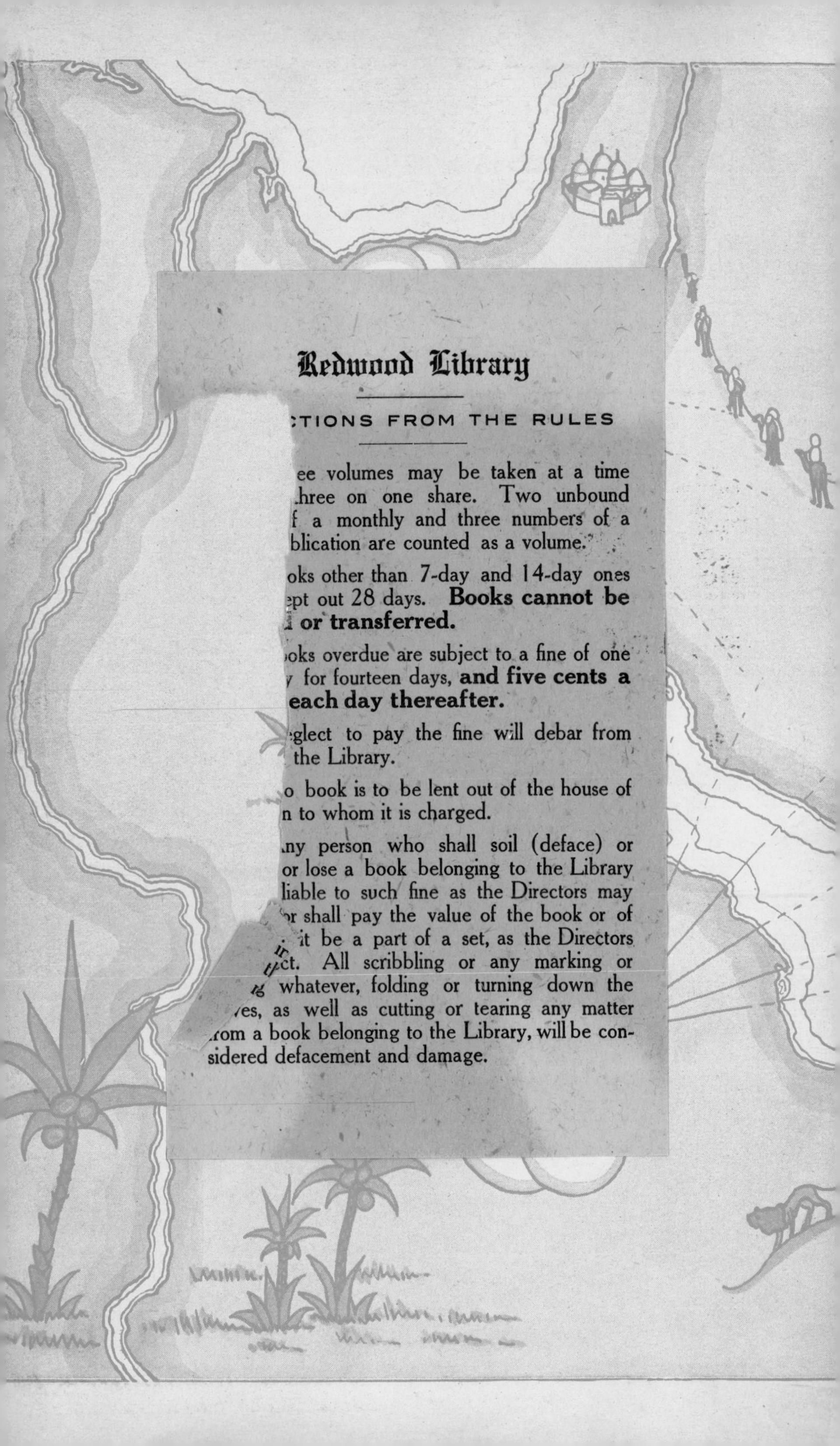